Watson Griffin

Twok

A Novel

Watson Griffin

Twok
A Novel

ISBN/EAN: 9783337028978

Printed in Europe, USA, Canada, Australia, Japan

Cover: Foto ©Thomas Meinert / pixelio.de

More available books at **www.hansebooks.com**

HAMILTON, ONT.
GRIFFIN & KIDNER.
1887

GRIFFIN & KIDNER, PRINTERS,
HAMILTON, ONT.

TWOK.

CHAPTER I.

WHY she was Twok, or who Twok was, Twok did not know. Sometimes she was not quite sure she was Twok at all, or anybody else. Then she would look at her hands and feet, pinch her cheeks and pull her hair, after which she would feel quite sure that she was somebody at all events, else why did it hurt so? Her earliest recollection was a very vivid one—so vivid that it seemed to obliterate all that went before. A little room with a low ceiling, dimly lighted by one window and heated by a wornout stove; a table in the centre covered with an assortment of odd dishes; in one corner a heap of baskets of all sizes and shapes, reaching almost to the ceiling; in another corner a bed on which lay an old man with a long gray beard, who seemed to be in great pain; sitting on a chair beside the bed a sallow-faced old woman. Twok had no recollection of her own place in the room, but knew her heart was aching because she could not ease the old man's pain. Turning uneasily on his bed, the old man raised himself on one elbow and looking eagerly into the eyes of the woman said,

"I would never have left her with you if it had not been for this accident, but if you do her any harm—if you teach her any wickedness—I'll haunt you, old woman, I'll haunt you every day of your life. I haven't made many prayers in my life—not enough to be bothersome—so 'I guess this one won't be refused. 'Taint like as if I'd been pesterin' Him with prayers mornin' and night till He got tired listenin' to me. I haven't asked for anything for years before, but ever since I knew this accident was goin' to kill me I have been prayin' that I might be able to haunt you if you do Twok any harm. And I'll do it, Meg, if I have to spend an eternity in hell to pay for it after you are in your grave."

The old woman tremblingly protested that she would not harm the child for the world.

"Then," he continued, "you'll find all I've got in a bag under those baskets. You may have half for keeping her and the rest is for her. You must——"

The sentence was never completed. The old man gasped for breath and fell back on his pillow, dead. There was another blank in Twok's memory after that. Meg's Rest was one of the most popular cheap lodging houses among the canals of Buffalo. The police always had their eyes on Meg, for although they had never detected any violation of the law they knew that she observed it rather from fear than from love, and her lodgers were not always of the most respectable class. Whether or not she believed that the old man would carry out his threat, she never tried to teach Twok any wickedness. She never asked her to lie, or beg, or steal, but endeavored on the contrary to check any such propensities by saying very often,

"If you do that, you'll have the Law on you."

Now, what the Law was Twok did not know, but it became the only terror of her life. She was not at all a timid child, but she had an unbounded dread of this awful, indefinite, vengeful Law. She had once seen a mad dog rushing by and had an impression that the Law was something like that only a thousand times as large. Twok's idea of Law was very like some people's idea of God. Of the fiercest and most wicked of ordinary men she had no fear, but she would hide in fright at the approach of policemen, for they were officers of the Law.

The rough men who frequented Meg's Rest were proud of Twok. They taught her to dance and sing, and when the little bare feet tapped the floor, while the lovely face was aglow and the blue eyes sparkled with pleasure at their praise, they would have killed anyone who offered to do her harm. Had she been older, they would not have hesitated to urge her to a life of shame and misery; but she was only a child then, and her purity and beauty made them mannerly in her presence. Perhaps after all their company was better for her at that time than that of the children of the neighborhood, whose young lives were already full of vileness. Meg kept Twok away from other children, never allowing her to play with them.

Many people have an unreasoning dislike of the use of the word "luck." They ascribe everything good and evil to God, and wonder greatly at the mysteries of Providence. Luck is the outcome of a combination of circumstances the result of design but not designed. Many different people design to bring about many different things. They act and react on one another and the result of their designing is a train of events bringing to one evil and to another good. Twok had a piece of good luck one day. She had no idea of her age but must have been about eight years old when passing a store she stopped to examine some gay goods displayed in front. Among other things was a bright red dress which greatly pleased her. Lifting it up she held it beside her own shabby dress. She had no intention of stealing—she knew that was against the Law; but the store-keeper coming out saw it in her hand and said,

"Ah, you little thief, I'll have the Law on you!"

She was off like a shot, still holding in her hand the dress which she had forgotten to lay down in her fright. The store-keeper ran after her, calling "stop thief," and soon a crowd was following. Twok never looked behind. She was fleet of foot, and as she heard the panting crowd in pursuit she thought the great mad Law was after her. Turning a corner sharply she ran against a tall man.

"Oh, ha! child," said he, "what's the matter?"

"The Law is after me."

He did not wait to question, but snatching her up ran swiftly across the street, darted down a lane and slipping into a doorway, closed the door with a bang. Then without stopping he walked slowly up a pair of winding stairs and opening a door at the top entered a room so small that there was only space for a single bed and a wash stand. Sitting down on the bed with Twok still in his arms he looked in silence first at her and then at the dress which she clasped tightly in her hand. At last he said,

"So you've been stealin', have you?"

"No," said Twok, dropping the dress and looking at it in dismay, "I didn't mean to. I was only lookin' at it."

"Well," said he, looking somewhat incredulous, "Who are you and where is your folks?"

"I'm all alone. I have nobody but myself."

"Don't you live with nobody?"

"Yes, I live with old Meg, but she don't belong to me."

"Meg of Meg's Rest?"

Twok nodded.

"Oh, I've heard of you. Do you want to go ho— back?"

Twok looked up at the man. He was thin and haggard and shabbily dressed, and would not have been considered attractive by most people; but there was a kindly look about the eyes and mouth that inspired confidence. She nestled up close in his arms as if sure of his protection and said,

"No. The Law might get me."

"Well, I'm an unlucky dog myself. Was born unlucky— always been unlucky, and you won't get much good from me, but you'll perhaps be better off than with her. Will you go with me?"

"Yes."

"Can you stand hunger?"

Twok nodded.

"And cold?"

Twok nodded again.

" And bein' tired ? "

" Yes."

" Well, then it's a bargain. Would you mind givin' me a kiss ? "—and he looked half apologetically down at the flushed little face. For answer she put her arms about his neck and kissed him, and then nestled down in his arms again.

" My name is Jake, " he said in a moment. " Same as you I have only one name. Never had no father. Leastways I never saw him and he never saw me. We'll both start fresh now. The first thing is to get out of this city. I think we'll steer across the line. That's where you came from, I've heard."

" Where ? "

" Canada. Meg told me that your granddad brought you from Montreal when you was a baby. We'll go there. I ain't never got no good in this country and no more have you. Perhaps we'll have better luck there."

CHAPTER II.

CANADA is cold in winter, but its summers are Italian. The first day that Twok and Jake spent together in Canada was a bright one. It was the first of June. The warm sunshine was evaporating the moisture of the last night's shower; the fruit trees were in blossom; the birds were singing; and all nature seemed to be joying in the sunshine.

"Don't you think," said Jake as they walked along the country roadside, "that it would be a good idea for us to have another name? Seems kinder more respectable to have two names."

"It would be nice," assented Twok, "but where will we get it?"

"There's lots of names to choose from," said Jake, "if I could only remember 'em all. You can get lots of 'em in a big city where there's signs, but the best place is a graveyard. You haven't no one to bother you there and can take your pick."

"Couldn't we make one ourselves?"

"Perhaps we could. I guess other people before us had to choose names, 'cause there's so many names. Must have been a lot of people born wrong."

"Born wrong?"

"Yes. Don't you see when they're born right they know who their father is and take the same name as him, but when they don't know, they have to choose new ones."

As they walked they turned an angle of the road and a little church, surrounded by a graveyard was in sight. In a few moments they came to it and walked among the tombstones, Jake reading the inscriptions aloud to Twok, who could not read. There were not many people buried there, and the names were simple enough. Two graves made close together attracted Twok's attention ; one was very long and the other very short.

"Just like you and me," said Twok to Jake.

The marble at the head of the long grave was in memory of Thomas Kelgwin ; that at the head of the short one commemorated his little daughter Bessie.

"Wouldn't they do?" asked Twok.

"I think they would," said Jake, and as he spoke two tears dropped from his eyes upon the head of the little girl beside him. That was Twok's baptism. Jake brushed the tears from his eyes and hurried away with the child. As he stood there beside the grave with Twok's hand in his, he thought of his past life. Nobody's son, born in a barn, reared in a foundling asylum, he had never known father or mother. Life had always presented its dark side to him ; he had always been unlucky. But that was not why he cried. Looking at the child's grave the thought came to him that the child at his side might die too, and what would become of her? What did she know of God and how could he teach her? And then the thought began to grow on Jake that he was not the proper person to have the guardianship of Twok. He must find someone who could teach her and guide her. He must give the child, whom he had learned in a few days to love dearly, to someone else. He had lived a lonely life—very lonely, with no one to love. The future without Twok would be still more lonely. That was why Jake cried.

They walked a little way in silence. Then Twok said,

"Oh, Jake, wouldn't it be as much against the Law to take somebody else's name as to take somebody's dress?"

"Why, I don't see what they want their names for after they're dead, but perhaps they mightn't like to have other people wearin' 'em around and disgracin' 'em. I guess we'd better make one."

"Let's put your name and mine together—Jaketwok. How would that do?" said Twok.

"People might guess that we made it ourselves. There's all sorts of names that anyone can take—Horse, Cow, Grass, Rake, Hoe, Spade, Fence. Why, I've met people with all sorts of names like that. There's lots to choose from."

"Suppose we changed Jaketwok a little Nobody would know we made it then. Say it fast and it sounds like Jakwok."

"That'll do first rate. Jake Jakwok and Twok Jakwok. They'll think you're my sister. But what would you say if I should give you to someone else?"

"No, Jake, you mustn't. I want to stay with you."

"It was a much used road by which they travelled, and at this moment a burly farmer with big red whiskers drove past on a woodrack. He looked curiously back at Twok, slowed up his horses and waited for them, saying,

"D'ye want a ride?"

They thankfully accepted.

"Where you going?"

"To Montreal."

"Long way. Ain't going to walk, are you?"

"I guess so."

"Guess the little girl'll be dead 'fore you get there. Your daughter?"

"No"

"Sister?"

"Well sorter like a sister."

"Kind of half sister, I suppose. I have a half sister myself. Ain't half as pretty as this one though. Where are you going to stay to-night?"

"I don't know much about this country," said Jake. "We just came here from the States. Do you think we could stop at some house all night? I might do some work to pay for it."

"Come home with me. I want some one to help me cut wood to-night to take to Hamilton to-morrow. You can ride on top of the load as far as Hamilton."

Twok listened to their conversation, and whenever a farmhouse came in sight she would say, "Is that your house?"

To this he always replied, "No, not yet." It's miles yet."

Twok thought it must be a hundred miles. she was so tired before the farmer said, "Here we are," and drove into a lane leading up to a large frame house which was painted red.

"Say, you forgot to tell me your names."

"My name," said Jake, "is Jake Jakwok."

"And mine," said Twok, "is Twok Jakwok."

"What queer names! Mine is common enough. John Stone. Easy to remember that, isn't it little girl? A stone is what you throw, but it takes a pretty strong man to throw me, I can tell you."

The horses stopped in front of the house and John Stone called out in a loud voice,

"Jennie, Jen—ee."

A freckled faced little girl with a tangled mass of red hair came out on the verandah and called back in just as loud a voice, John, John—ee." What do you want with Jen—ee? You don't need to yell the roof of the house off."

"Don't be cross, Jennie. Here's a little girl come all the way from the States to see you. Take her into the house and give her something to eat."

John Stone gave the reins to Jake, and jumping down himself lifted Twok from the wagon and set her on the verandah beside Jennie. Then he drove away with Jake.

"Come into the house," said Jennie. "John and I are keeping house together because mother and pa and Maria Ann have gone to aunt Sarah's wedding. They won't be home until to-morrow. John says its a busy time, too, and I think it's a shame to leave us here alone. Don't you?"

Twok not knowing the merits of the case said that it was "real mean," and Jennie taking her hand led her into the house.

"What lovely hair you have!" said Jennie, "I wish mine was like that. But why don't you wear a hat? The sun will bleach all the pretty color out of it."

"I haven't any hat."

"What funny people they must be in the States! Is that your Sunday dress?"

Twok not knowing what sort of a dress a Sunday dress was, but supposing it must mean a brightly colored dress, said,

"No, I haven't any Sunday dress. The one that I had in my hand when the Law chased me was very pretty, but Jake made me leave it because it wasn't mine."

"I should think he would if it wasn't yours. I wouldn't want to wear anybody else's dress. Do you like bread and milk?"

The big bowl of milk that Jennie set on the table looked very tempting indeed to Twok, and she eagerly assented.

"What did you do to get rid of your freckles?" said Jennie, as she watched Twok eating.

"I never had any."

"How lucky you are! I've tried everything. Jim Dace told me to put on a little vinegar and then rub it with sandpaper. It nearly took the skin off and I'm going to pay him back some day. I'm using buttermilk for them now."

"Do they hurt much?"

"What?"

"Freckles."

"No, you silly! They don't hurt at all, but they make me look ugly."

"I don't think you're ugly. I think you look nice."

"Do you? It's nice of you to say so. How old are you?"

"I don't know."

"Well, I don't think you know very much. Why doesn't your mother teach you?"

"I haven't any mother. I never had one."

"Oh, that makes a difference. My mother has taught me an awful lot. Does your pa teach you?"

"I haven't any pa."

"If you had a mother she'd tell you things. I'm eleven. You're about as big as I was when I was eight. Why don't you eat the rest of your bread and milk? Don't you like it?"

"Yes, but I'm keepin' it for Jake."

"Oh, you needn't do that. There's lots more for him when he comes in. Here they come now. Are you hungry, John?"

John said he was hungry and that he knew Jake was hungry and was sure they'd both starve if Jennie didn't hurry up supper. Jennie hurried and in ten minutes they all sat down together, Twok eating as heartily as if she had not had a bowl of bread and milk beforehand.

"Did you ever see United States Grant?" said Jennie as she passed a cup of tea to Jake.

"No," said Jake

"Well, I would if I lived in the States," said Jennie, "because I read in a newspaper that General United States Grant was the greatest man living in America. Do they call him United States Grant because he stopped the rebellion and saved the United States?"

Jake shook his head ignorantly and looked somewhat confused.

"I told her," said John, "that U. S. just stood for some name of his, perhaps Uriah Samuel, but she wouldn't believe me. She said she learned at school that U. S. always stood for United States."

"Oh," said Jake, "you mean General Grant. His first name is Ulysses, but I ain't no hand at readin' and I've never heard what his second name is. It's funny some people has three names and others has a bother gettin' more 'n one."

"You had better go to bed at once, little girl, for we're going to start early in the morning," said John after tea was over, as he went out with Jake to load up the wood.

"What is your name?" asked Jennie, after the men had gone out.

"Twok Jakwok."

"Well, you're a queer one every way. You have a funny name. You don't have any hat and you don't wear any shoes and you haven't any freckles, nor any mother nor any pa, and you don't know how old you are."

"I may get some freckles after I live in Canada for a while," said Twok, in the tone of one excusing herself for some great fault and promising to do better in the future.

Jennie was so astonished at this reply that she let a saucer drop on the floor.

"Now see what you made me do," she cried.

"Oh, I'm so sorry," said Twok, "I didn't mean to. Can't it be mended? There used to be an old man at Meg's who would break saucers on purpose to mend 'em. He'd fasten 'em together with some stuff he had in a bottle and then he'd fasten an iron weight on and hold it up to show that the saucer was mended tight."

"There was a peddler came here with some, but mother wouldn't buy any. I guess she'll wish she had when she comes home, for this is the second saucer I've broken since she went away. But I don't care. She should have taken me to the wedding. John said you were to go to bed. If your feet were not so dirty, I'd let you sleep with me."

"Couldn't I wash them?"

"I guess you'd better. Here's a towel and soap and there's a tin wash-dish out by the cistern. Don't you fall in, now, when you're pulling up the water."

Twok found the wash-dish, and as there was water in the tin pail by the cistern she did not have to draw any up. In a few minutes she entered the kitchen again and said,

"Now will I do?"

"Yes, you're as clean as can be, but I guess you can have a bed to yourself, because all the folks are away and Maria Ann says nobody can sleep with me because I roll around so."

So Twok had a very soft bed all to herself that night and did not wake up until Jennie called her, saying,

"Hurry up! John wouldn't let me call you before. It's time you were off."

There was just time for Twok to eat a bowl of bread and milk and put some cakes in her pocket before John and Jake were ready to start. Jake lifted Twok up to John, who sat on top of the wood, and John put her down on a buffalo robe and told her to hold on tight. Then Jake climbed up and sat down beside her, and they were off. Jennie ran after them to say to Twok,

"I forgot to kiss you good-bye. You must come and see me again."

Twok nodded and smiled, and away they went.

Long before they reached Hamilton they met a gentleman who said,

"Hello, John, where are you going?"

"To Hamilton."

"I'll save you the trouble if you'll sell it to me at the same rate as the last. I'm almost out."

"It's a bargain," said John turning his horses around. "I guess you two will have to go on alone."

They parted with John Stone with many thanks and promises to call and see him if they ever passed that way again.

"I'd ask you to stay and work for us only we've got all we can use when we are all at home," said John as he drove away.

"This looks like a pretty road," said Twok, as they came to a cross road. "Let us go this way."

The road did not lead to Hamilton, but Jake not knowing which way to turn followed Twok's advice. They walked until Twok was very tired, and then sat down by the roadside. In a few moments Jake saw a wagon coming and they went out to the road to ask for a ride. The driver was drunk, but said they could get on if they liked. So Jake lifted Twok up and asked if the road led to Hamilton.

"Yer goin' to Hamilton?"

"Yes," said Jake.

"This'll take yer straighter'n an arrow," said the driver, after which he paid no further attention to them until they had gone several miles. Then turning to Twok he said,

"Yer goin' to Hamilton?"

"Yes," said Twok.

"Well, what yer comin' this way for? This ain't the road to Hamilton."

"Why you said it was," said Jake.

"No, I didn't. This is the road to Linklater. That's what I said. Linklater's better place'n Hamilton!"

"Let us off then."

"What's good goin' part way? Like swimmin' back after gettin' half way cross river. Better go all way."

As he did not stop Jake thought they might as well sit still and go on to Linklater. Half an hour afterward the horses turned their heads up a lane and the driver arousing himself said,

"That's the road to Linklater, straight on."

Jake knew Twok was tired, and he would have asked for a night's lodging if the man had been sober, but under the circumstances he thought it best to walk on, and they continued on their way until they came to a wood.

"Are you tired enough to sleep in the woods to-night, Twok?" said Jake.

"Yes, anywhere."

Entering the wood they found a sheltered mossy spot, and after they had eaten some of the cakes with which Twok's pocket was filled Jake made a bed of his coat, and Twok pillowing her head on his arm went to sleep. It was quite early, but they slept soundly until morning, when Jake, telling Twok to remain there until he returned, started off to buy something for breakfast.

CHAPTER III.

"I say, boys. Here comes old Carlock. Let's have some fun with him."

The speaker was a large, rather handsome but rough-looking boy of fourteen years of age, who stood among a crowd of boys who were going to school, but had stopped on the way to play marbles. An old man was coming along the road, feeling each step of the way before him with a cane. He was very thin, but had apparently at one time been very fat, for his clothes hung loosely upon him and his skin seemed to be looser than his clothes. It hung in a sort of bag below his chin, where it looked very like a monkey's pouch.

"Hello, old monkey!" cried the big boy as he switched off the old man's hat with a long pole and threw it into a puddle of water.

"Get along, old baldhead!" cried the boys as the shining top of the old man's head was revealed by the loss of his hat. He trembled violently, straightened himself up and for a moment looked strong and vigorous as he pointed his cane at the boys and cursed them. Then he looked about as if expecting that something fearful would befall them, but the birds sang on just as sweetly as if their harmony had not been disturbed by that curse; the air was just as full of fragrance; the sun that shines alike upon the just and the unjust shone on as brightly as ever; and no bears came out of the wood to devour those wicked children. Instead a blue-eyed, golden-haired, barefooted, bareheaded little girl sprang out from a neighboring thicket and placing herself beside the old man, cried out,

"Don't you dare to touch him!"

It was Twok.

"My! but she's a beauty," cried the big boy; "say, sissy, give us a kiss and we'll let old Carlock go."

The other boys looked on in amazement and the old man picking up his hat, hobbled off without thanking the child for her interference or waiting to see what would come of it. Twok looked at the big boy scornfully and said,

"You're a mean, wicked boy. I hate you."

He sprang forward and caught her, saying,

"Gimme a kiss and I'll let you go."

Twok struggled in vain to get away while the other boys looked half inclined to interfere in her behalf, and would probably have done so had not assistance arrived from another quarter. They stood at the foot of a hill, and just at this moment a horseman came to the top of the hill, and seeing what was going on below rode furiously toward them and leaping from his horse cried out,

"If you don't let that child alone, Sam Slemmings, I'll break every bone in your body."

Sam released her, and she, with one grateful glance at her deliverer, darted away. The young man who arrived so opportunely was tall and well formed, with dark hair, blue eyes, dark enough to be mistaken for black, and clearly cut features. He had a nervous habit of constantly twisting one shoulder as if it hurt him, and the movement of the shoulder was accompanied by a corresponding twitching of the mouth in the same direction.

"What business is it of yours, Joy Cougles, who I kiss?"

"I'll make it my business to thrash you within an inch of your life if you ever touch that child again."

The other boys had already started on a run for the schoolhouse, ashamed of their part in the proceedings, and as Sam walked off, Joy Cougles pursued his way on horseback, meditating on the depravity of human nature as exemplified in Sam Slemmings.

"The boy is a brute," he said to himself. "They say man was created in the image of God and that every man has some touch of the divine nature. I don't see where it comes in in Sam. A person can, I suppose, become more like God every day if he tries hard enough. I wonder would a fellow who never cultivated the divine part of him, but always indulged his animal propensities, become a mere animal at last. Suppose Sam should lose his spiritual nature and become a beast. I don't know that there is anything unreasonable in such a supposition. I am sure my dog Lion is worth a dozen such as Sam."

Meanwhile Twok had returned to the place where Jake left her and found him there looking very anxious.

"Why, Twok, where have you been? I've been looking all over for you."

"I got tired of waitin' for you and went out to the road to look for you. I saw a lot of mean boys teasin' an old man and I was goin' to make 'em stop, and then one of 'em caught me; but a good man came along and stopped him."

"I wish I could have seen the rascal," said Jake. "But come, you must be hungry. Sit down on this," and he spread his coat on the grass. The two sat down on the coat and ate heartily of the simple meal which Jake had brought in a basket. When they had finished eating Jake said,

"Twok, I'm afraid I'll have to give you away."

"Oh, please don't. I'll be very good."

"Well, I've been unlucky since my birth, and there ain't no manner of use draggin' you down just because I'm down myself."

"What is the use of having the same name if we don't stay together?"

"Well, I don't know nothin', and you'll grow up a good-for-nothin' ignoramus if you stay with me."

"I don't care if I do," said Twok.

"Well, but you'll never get half enough to eat."

"I don't care," said Twok, defiantly; "I don't mind bein' hungry so very much."

"Would you like to be wicked and ugly like Meg when you grow up?"

"No."

"Well, you will unless you learn somethin'. I can't teach you much. Besides, I might die some day, and then you wouldn't have nobody; but if I give you away now, you will learn a lot of things and grow up to be a good woman. Then perhaps I'll strike luck some day and come back and get you."

"Who are you goin' to give me to?" said Twok, beginning to cry.

"I don't know yet, but I'll find someone that's good and wise. You must stay here alone to-day, Twok. I'll leave the basket with you, and if you get hungry you can eat. You can catch butterflies if you like, but you mustn't chase them far, because I want to find you here when I come back. It will be better for you to rest to-day. Your little feet are blistered."

"I don't want to chase butterflies. That would be as bad as the Law chasin' me. What right has a big thing like me got to chase a little thing like that?"

As Jake did not feel himself equal to this question he evaded it and said good-bye. That day was a weary one to Twok. She was left to amuse herself, and found it a rather difficult task. But in the evening Jake came, and they slept in the woods again as on the night before; but the air was chilly and they did not sleep at all soundly. Next morning the sky was overcast, and Jake said it would rain before night. It was very cold, too, for that time of the year, and so they took breakfast in a barn. After breakfast he made a bed in the hay mow, and they remained there while a cold rain fell outside. But in the evening the farmer, a rough man with a cross voice, finding them there, said that he would set his dog on them if they did not clear out. They went out into the rain, and Jake told Twok that he had found a pleasant home for her with people who would teach her to be a good woman. An hour later they were standing, drenched to the skin, outside a very cheery-looking building, the windows of which seemed full of light to the wet and tired and hungry little girl.

CHAPTER IV.

THE village of Linklater is situated on one of the highest points of a ridge of high land which stretches for some distance along the north-western shore of Lake Ontario. Linklater village at the time our story begins was not a busy place, and it did not look as busy as it was, for most of the business was at the mills, which were down by the creek in the ravine, out of sight of passers-by. Besides these mills there were a blacksmith's shop, half a dozen stores and about as many taverns. The churches were on side streets and most of the well-to-do people of the place lived in the outskirts of the village, the center being mostly occupied by the workmen at the mills, whose houses were not very well kept, because, as Joy Cougles said, most of their spare time was spent at the village tavern, so that anyone passing through the village along the main road was apt to form an unfavorable opinion of it. It was not a cheerful place either. There had been a time when the people thought it would one day be a city, but this belief had long since ceased to prevail. The more energetic residents had left; the railway had passed it by, and Linklater had sunk into a kind of lethargy. There were never many people to be seen on the streets, and those who were seen looked sleepy. Even the stores had an air of drowsy gloominess about them calculated to make the most brisk and cheery person melancholy. But there was one place in the village which never seemed to be impressed by the general gloominess, but rather shone the brighter in its cheery good-humor beside its morose companions. This was the shop of Joy Cougles, the village blacksmith. It was built of red brick, and the sun in rising and setting seemed to take peculiar delight in singling it out and shedding upon its red walls a golden glory. It sent its beams through the window, too, at these times, and joined the fire within in casting a ruddy light on the face of Joy, as he dealt strong blows on the glowing iron or stooped to read by the light of the fire a passage from some old author, for Joy was an Elihu Burritt in a small way, and always had a book beside him. But it was not merely on sunshiny days that this blacksmith's shop looked cheerful, for the very things that made the rest of Linklater village dreary seemed to make this place more cheery, the outside cloudiness and chilliness serving but to make the bright fire look brighter and bring out in warmer colors the warmth and comfort within. Joy's friends were divided into two parties, the one contending that it was the shop that made Joy cheery, and the other that it was Joy who made the shop so; but all united in saying that they could never enjoy the place half so well if anyone else were its master. And yet there was nothing merry about Joy. He never joked and seldom said anything laughable. The secret of his cheerfulness seemed to be a spirit of contentment that made him whistle as he worked, and gave to his face a brightness of expression which sometimes almost cast a halo around it. But it had not always been thus, for in early childhood Joy had a violent temper, and had only been able to overcome it by hard fighting and much prayer. Occasionally there came a flash of the old devil, as he called it, and then Joy's face twitched nervously and he twisted his shoulder as if in pain. This twitching and twisting was a nervous weakness which he always exhibited when strongly excited.

Joy's father had started as a lawyer in Linklater many years before with bright prospects. Young, handsome, eloquent, he was received with favor everywhere, and was regarded as a good match by fond mamas and their sweet daughters. Everybody was astonished one day when he introduced as his wife the little crippled daughter of Tim Somers, the village blacksmith, a pretty, patient girl of sixteen, whom everybody loved and pitied. Overlooking her crippled limbs, Minna Somers was the superior of any girl in Linklater. She had a lovely face and a well-cultivated mind, for she had always had a taste for reading, which was encouraged by her mother and humored by her father. She was so patient and so pretty that everyone was interested in her. The ladies of the village brought her flowers and lent her books, and were not displeased to find that she knew more about both flowers and books than they did. Still, no one thought she was a suitable wife for Lawyer Cougles, and the marriage caused much gossip, which ended in the ladies transferring their pity to the young lawyer. During the first three years of their married life he was very attentive to his crippled wife, and although his practice was not very remunerative, they lived happily together in their pretty house. But he was very fond of company and very fond of wine. The cripple could not accompany him in his visits, and after a time he left her very much alone, excusing himself by saying that success in his profession depended upon his cultivation of acquaintances. Everyone was pleased to see him come: everyone was sorry to have him go; for the same cheerfulness that afterward exhibited itself in a softer form in Joy characterized the father and made him the life of the company he frequented. And everywhere he went they brought out wine, for temperance principles had not made such headway then as now. One night, after making several calls and exciting himself with wine, he started for home alone; his horse ran away, and a few hours afterwards he was carried home to his wife, to die with her arms around him, reproaching himself for his folly and asking forgiveness of her. He had always been kind to her, even when the worse for liquor, and now he called his five-year-old boy, Joy, to him and said,

"Joy, your father is dying now. You will never see him

any more. Your mother will have no one to care for her but you. She is a little mother and very weak; you must take care of her when you are big and strong. You must care for the little mother better than father did, and you cannot do it if you ever taste liquor. You must never drink it, Joy."

The little mother was sobbing now, and Joy sobbed too, as his father closed his eyes in death. Joy never forgot those dying words. Almost a baby in years, he became a man in his sense of responsibility. Tim Somers, a rugged, honest, hard working man, took his daughter home and taught her boy his trade. Some of the lawyer's furniture and most of his books were removed to the house of the blacksmith, the remainder being sold.

Joy worked hard at his trade and studied as he worked, so that when the old man died the boy was able to conduct the business himself. He had never ceased to watch over the little mother. She was weaker than ever now, but he was tall and strong. Her limbs were withered and useless, but his muscles were strong as steel, and he carried her about as he would a little child. Weak and crippled though she was, there were women with less of happiness in their lives than the little mother. And perhaps after all it was from her that Joy got his cheerfulness. He thought so himself, and often said that the most discontented man on earth must become cheerful, could he see the bright face of his patient mother as often as he did. It was a lovely face to look upon. She was only thirty-seven and looked much younger, in spite of all her suffering. Her beautiful brown hair fell over her shoulders like a school girl's and reached far below the waist. She wore it so to please Joy, who liked to note the surprise of strangers when informed that the lovely little girl with the long brown hair was his mother. Oh, Joy was proud of the little mother and she was proud of him. The house of the young blacksmith was in the rear of the shop. There were only five rooms. That of the mother was large and pleasant, with a fire-place at one end and two windows at the other. It was nicely carpeted, well furnished, and presented a most inviting appearance; but what Joy and his mother were proudest of was the father's well filled bookcase. The mother's room had been the dining and sitting room until old man Somers died. Then Joy said that she, who must remain in the room so much of the time, should have the most pleasant room in the house, and so a change was made. Joy's room was a small one; he had slept there with his grandfather for many years, and if the old man could have returned he would have found the room just the same as ever. There was nothing there to indicate that the tastes of the young blacksmith were different from those of the old one. Joy never smoked, but the old man's pipes and tobacco were there as he left them. There were no books excepting those which the old man left, and every article of furniture was still in its old place. Joy had a fancy that since Tim Somers would never have anything moved during his lifetime, he might not like to have changes made after he was dead. But Joy did not find the brightness of his life in that bedroom. When not at work he was usually in his mother's room, sometimes reading to her, sometimes reading to himself, and often wrapt in deep thought.

One June night, when the year seemed to have forgotten that it was summer time, or to have taken suddenly to shivering at the thought of the next winter, Joy sat before the fire in his shop. Outside a dismal rain was falling and a cold wind dashed the drops against the window panes, but the shop within looked as cheery as usual. He had rubbed his mother's head until she was soothed to sleep before he left her, and afraid to work lest the noise might awaken her, he gazed musingly into the fire. His reverie was interrupted by a timid rap at the door, and leaving the fire, to open the door, he admitted Twok.

She stood there hesitatingly until he offered his hand. Then she took it trustingly and he led her to the fire.

"It is very cold," he said, "and you are very wet. What brings you here on such a night as this?"

She stretched her little hands before the fire and said with a shiver, "because Jake has given me to you."

"Given you to me!" said Joy in astonishment. "Why does he give you to me?"

Something big came up in Twok's throat. She tried to choke it down, but it would come, and then the tears that she tried so hard to keep back burst from her eyes and she put up her little hands to hide them. Joy couldn't stand that. He took her in his arms, smoothed down the golden hair and said,

"Never mind; don't cry. I'm very glad to have you come. Where is your home, dear, and what is your name?"

"I haven't any home, but my name is Twok," said the child, taking her hands from her face, resting one on Joy's shoulder and brushing away the tears with the other. You see I lived with Meg in Buffalo. She was bad and the Law was always tryin' to get her. I didn't belong to her, but my granddad died and I had to live with her. One day I was lookin' at a pretty dress, and I didn't mean to steal it; but the man in the store set the Law on me, and it chased me until Jake picked me up and carried me to his room so the Law couldn't get me; and then he brought me here."

"Did you not wish to stay with Jake? Was he not kind to you?"

"Yes, he was kind to me, but he said that little girls grow to be women, and if they don't learn a lot, they're bad like Meg. He said he didn't know how to teach me 'cause he didn't know enough himself, but he said you could."

"Perhaps he is right, Twok," said Joy. "I cannot teach you very much myself, but I have a little mother who is the best of women. You will be my little sister, and she will teach you to be a good woman."

"Have you a mother?" said Twok. "Oh, I'm so glad."

Then Joy tip-toed softly to his mother's room and brought out a night-dress, saying,

"I will go away for a little while. You must take off your damp clothes by the fire and put on this night-dress while I am gone. When I come back I will show you to bed."

Joy went to his room and, opening the bed, smoothed down the pillows. Then going to the dining-room he soon returned with a tray of eatables, which he offered to Twok, who sat on a chair before the fire, arrayed in the little mother's night-dress, her own clothes at her feet.

"Are you hungry?" he asked.

"Yes," said Twok.

He watched her while she ate, and when she had finished said, "you will have to sleep in my bed to-night, my little sister. I will sleep here by the fire."

"No; you mustn't," said Twok. "Let me sleep here. I'm used to sleepin' anywhere now."

But Joy took her in his arms, carried her softly to his bed, tucked in the covers and went back to the fire again, not to sleep, but to muse over his strange little visitor, and wonder whether he had acted wisely in accepting such a great responsibility without consulting his mother.

"The child is lovely," he said to himself, "and her evil surroundings do not seem to have done her any harm. She is truthful and trustful, if I mistake not; and I think she will be very faithful to those whom she learns to love. The little mother needs a daughter, I need a sister, and she needs both mother and brother. Poor little Twok! I know not whether God ever directs our footsteps; if so, he must have brought you here. O Heavenly Father, whether she comes by Thy guidance or only by chance, help me and my mother to lead her rightly toward that pure womanhood which she seeks."

CHAPTER V.

WHEN Twok awoke next morning, the first thing she noticed was her clothing on a chair at the foot of the bed. She jumped out of bed immediately and dressed herself, wondering what new experience she was to have that day, for there had been so many changes of late that she was prepared for almost anything. Now Jake had been greatly troubled about Twok's ignorance, and had tried in his simple way to teach her what he knew. His only prayer was, "Now I lay me down to sleep." This he taught her, and told her to say it every morning and every night.

"But," said Twok, "if I say 'now I lay me down to sleep' when I'm gettin' up, that will be tellin' a lie, won't it?"

Jake rather thought it would, and said perhaps she had better only say it at night; but Twok thought she could change it to suit the hour of day, and so when Joy Cougles rapped at the door that morning, and hearing no response, opened it a little way, intending to call her, he saw the child on her knees at the bed and heard a sweet voice say,

"Now I'm gettin' out of bed, I pray the Lord my soul to keep; and if I die before the night, I pray the Lord my soul to take."

Then Twok came to the door, and taking Joy's hand went with him to his mother's room. Joy had told his mother all about Twok and now he led the child to the bed, saying, "Mother, I have brought you a daughter."

The cripple held out her arms for the child, whom Joy lifted gently and laid on the bed beside her, and then Twok was clasped to that motherly bosom as she had never been clasped by any one before, and the pale, sweet face of the patient, cheerful little woman and the sun-burned face of the motherless child lay close together on the pillow for a long time. They were both lovely faces, Joy thought, as he looked down on them for a few moments before leaving them alone. Such a quiet, restful feeling came over Twok then. She had at last found a home and a mother. Often during her wanderings with Jake she had seen old hens gathering the little chickens under their wings, and had almost envied the little ones. Now she thought of the little chickens and wondered if they felt as she did. She was sure they could not be any happier, for had she not a mother too? After a while the cripple said,

"Kiss me dear and then help me to dress. Mary has always done it, for I am very weak and helpless; but now that I have a daughter I can be already dressed when she comes. Mary Slemmings is a kind girl who comes every day to help us with the work. Joy gets the breakfast himself, and he is a very good cook. He and Mary will have to teach you to cook, for I want you to be my little housekeeper. Mary will, no doubt, be married some day, and then she will have her husband to care for."

Twok paid great attention to the directions given and dressed the little woman almost as quickly as Mary could have done. Before many months passed she could attend to all the wants of the cripple with a tender skill that even the gentle Mary could not equal. And Twok and Mary became great friends. Mary did feel a little hurt at first, when she found that Twok was to take her place as waitress on Mrs. Cougles, but she soon became reconciled to the change and learned to love the child dearly. A pretty girl was Mary Slemmings, and as good as she was pretty. Not a bit like her handsome but cruel brother Sam, not a bit like her father, Butcher Slemmings, who was fast making his fortune selling meat to the villagers and the people of the town in the valley below. Getting rich so fast, in fact, that he began to think his daughter was demeaning herself by working for wages in the house of the village blacksmith. He would have thought it very much worse, however, if she had offered to work without wages, as she wished to do. After all, he said, he needed all the money he could save just then to buy land in Toronto. Every dollar so invested would double itself in a few years he was sure. He was not quite so well satisfied with his investments in Hamilton, but still he was confident that he would lose nothing there. He would move to Toronto or Montreal after he had made his fortune, and nobody there would know what he or his children had done in Linklater village.

Joy's dog Lion had a great dislike for both the butcher and his son Sam, and always showed his teeth when he saw them. His dislike for Sam was so great that he refused to take a very tempting looking piece of meat which the boy offered him as he passed Joy's shop a few days after Twok's arrival. Twok, who was watching the dog and the boy from the window, called to Joy,

"There's Mary's bad brother tryin' to coax your dog away."

Joy hurried anxiously to the door. Sam had passed on after throwing the meat to the dog. Lion looked after Sam to see that he wasn't looking, and then hastily swallowed the meat. Joy called him into the shop, saying,

"Come in, old fellow; I hope that meat wasn't poisoned."

It was poisoned, and Lion died in agony in a very short time, looking with appealing eyes to his master for relief. Joy knelt beside him even after he was dead, and seemed to be so grief-stricken that Twok crept into his arms and said,

"I just come in time to take his place. You can love me instead of Lion."

That did comfort him greatly and he said, "I do love you, my dear little Twok, better than Lion already; but he was such a good dog and seemed to know so much, that I can't help feeling sorry. Nor can I help thinking that his life is worth more than Sam's. If ever a dog deserved to have a future life, my Lion did, and hanging would not be too great punishment for the boy who killed him."

Joy made a coffin for his dog while Twok looked on, and they buried him in a vacant lot adjoining the shop. Joy found a large stone, which he placed on the grave, and on the stone he carved,

"Here lies a dog that was almost a man, murdered by a boy who is almost a beast."

Sam, prowling around one night, found the stone and tried to roll it away, but it was too heavy for him and remained there for years.

CHAPTER VI.

"YOUR hammer sounds as if it were talking," said Twok to Joy one morning, as she stood watching him at his work.

"Do you think it does, Twok? Can you tell me what it says?"

"Something with three words, I know, because you hammer three times, then stop just about long enough to say 'Oh' and then hammer three times again. I'm sure it's saying something."

"It is saying something, Twok. You are the first person that ever found it out. I told Doctor Somerville myself one day, or he would never have known. I wish you could guess what the three words are."

"I can't guess. Please tell me. Sometimes you hammer more than three words. You make it say lots of different things."

"Just now it was saying, 'God is love.' I love my mother very much. I loved my dog Lion before he died, and I love you now. Are you learning to love me a little?"

"More than I can tell."

"Well, Twok, God loves us all more than we can tell, more than we can think."

"If you know that anyone loves you very much, you can't help loving back," said Twok.

"What a clever little girl you are, Twok. You see things yourself without being taught. That is just what I was going to say to you. So you see if we really think how much God loves us, we can't help loving back. Now I'm going to make the hammer say something else. Listen for a while and then guess."

"There are five words, I know, but I'm sure I can't guess. Do tell "

"A stroke of the hammer doesn't always mean a word. Sometimes it is only part of a word. As much of a word as you can hammer out in one stroke is a syllable. Some words have only one syllable. Others have two or three or even more. If a word has three syllables, it takes three strokes to hammer it out. What the hammer says now is, 'God is everywhere' Some people think of God as living up in the sky, looking down at us. But God is everywhere. You cannot think of any place where God is not. When you think of God always say to yourself, 'God is everywhere, and He loves us all and wants us to love each other.' Listen again to what the hammer says."

"Three syllables this time."

"Yes, and three words too. They are all words of one syllable. The hammer says, 'God is good.' God is good, and He wants you to be good. If you pray to Him He will help you to be good. You can pray in the middle of the day as well as at morning and night, and you don't need to get on your knees or shut your eyes or even open your mouth. You can just say down in your heart, 'God help me to be good.' He can tell what your heart says; He can feel what your heart says, as well as He can hear what your mouth says. Whenever you feel naughty ask the Great God, who is everywhere and never stops thinking about you, to help you to be good."

"Is the hammer always talking about God?"

"No. Sometimes I study with it. I make it say over the Greek verbs a great many times so I can't forget them, and sometimes it hammers enunciations in Euclid for me. You don't know what I mean now and you're too little to learn, but some day I will teach you. Would you like me to make it say something about you?"

"Oh, please do."
"Can you guess what it says?"
"No. Tell me."
"Twok, you are very pretty."
"Does God like to look at pretty people?"
"I don't know, Twok, but I do."
"I don't see why He makes some people ugly and other people pretty. Do you think that if God looked at an ugly little girl very hard for a long time, it would make her pretty?"
"It is a very hard question for me to answer, Twok. I rather think it would, but it would depend upon how He looked at her. He is looking at us in a certain way all the time."
"When I look at anybody very long my face seems to me to be changing to look like theirs. I saw a poor girl with such queer eyes when you took me to Sunday school, and I believe if I'd looked at her a minute longer my eyes would have turned like her's. I almost felt them changing and put my hands over them to shut out the sight."

Twok learned many lessons from the hammer after that, and was always a little wiser when the lesson was over than when it began. Joy was generally wiser, too, for the child's questions often set him upon a new train of thought. Twok learned from Mrs. Cougles as well as from Joy, and even Mary sometimes taught her. She listened to their talk, noticed how they pronounced their words and how they expressed themselves, and when she had been with them a year she was at least as well informed as most girls of her age. Mary before going home always read to Twok a chapter in the Bible, to which the child listened attentively, sometimes asking questions that Mary answered in a way that would have given the utmost satisfaction to Mr. Jackson, the Methodist minister whose church she attended regularly, but which did not always satisfy Joy, who listened somewhat anxiously. He wished that Mary would leave the child to his teaching, which was not altogether orthodox. But Joy would not hurt Mary's feelings by even hinting that he would prefer to teach Twok himself. One day after dinner was ready and while Joy was washing his hands, Mary read the story of how Esau sold his birthright to Jacob for a mess of pottage.

"I think," said Twok who had listened to the story with wide open eyes, "that Jacob was damn mean, don't you?"

The gentle Mary was horrified, and without a moment's thought slapped the child's face with her hand. The next moment Twok was gone. Joy had heard the question and the answer, and when he saw Mary slap Twok's face and the child rush from the house, his shoulder began to twist and his mouth to twitch, and Mary knew that he was angry.

"Oh, I'm so sorry!" she cried; "but she swore awfully, and I couldn't help it. I didn't think she was so wicked."

"Nothing wicked about her," said Joy. "I say that Jacob was damn mean, too. You don't know what swearing is, if you call that swearing. It isn't nice; it isn't ladylike; it isn't proper, because it isn't good English, and I have already told Twok not to make use of the expression. She is trying hard to speak correctly, but when she gets excited she occasionally makes a slip. She'll soon get over that. But, really, what's the harm in saying 'damn'? It may be used vindictively as a curse. That is wrong, of course—decidedly wrong; but it isn't swearing even then. To curse and to swear is to do two distinct things. Half the wrong conceptions people have are the result of a misunderstanding of language, and in this case a very clear command of Jesus is disregarded altogether, because people misunderstand the meaning of the word 'swearing.'"

"Didn't Jesus say, 'Swear not at all'?" asked Mary, timidly and tearfully.

"Yes, and you do it almost every day, just because you don't know what he meant by swearing."

"Oh, Joy, I never swore in my life."

"Yes, I have often heard you swear. You say, 'Upon

my word and honor.' That is really swearing. To swear is to endeavor to strengthen your word by appealing or referring to something else, as if your reputation for truthfulness would not support what you say. The Jews thought a man's word was valueless unless he strengthened it by appealing to something sacred, but Jesus thought it better to tell the simple truth rather than to swear by your word or honor or anything else. When Jesus said, 'Let your communication be yea, yea; nay, nay, for whatsoever is more than these cometh of evil,' he simply meant, 'Your word should be sufficient. Speak the truth and don't try to enforce belief by oaths or asseverations. These are not necessary, if you are known always to speak the truth.' I have never heard Twok swear since she came here. She always tells the simple truth and doesn't think it necessary to swear upon her honor or anything else. To curse a person is to wish that evil may befall that person. The word 'damn,' which strictly means to condemn, is often used in curses, and so it has become a sort of disreputable word that doesn't sound well in good company, but there is nothing wicked in the word itself. As Twok uses it, it is nothing but a strengthening adverb, no more harmful than the word 'awfully,' which I've often heard you use in the same way; only 'damn' is a more forcible word than 'awfully,' which has been almost worn out by silly school girls. Doctor Somerville has a bad habit of saying 'by Jingo,' very often. It's a foolish habit, but there is no harm in it. He doesn't use it as an asseveration. It is merely an exclamation, no more harmful than the exclamation 'oh!' And yet I heard Mr. Jackson reprove him for swearing the other day. He seems to think that the use of the word 'by' in an exclamation makes an oath, but the fact is that Jesus in his reference to swearing did not use the word 'by' at all. In the language in which he spoke the idea was expressed by an inflexion. I never use such expressions myself. It is a waste of words, and words are too good to be spoiled by that sort of usage; but it isn't swearing. To take God's name in vain is very wrong. It is worse than swearing by far, I think; but it isn't swearing, although many people call it so. It is blasphemy. Swearing, cursing and blasphemy are three different things, you see, although curses are often blasphemous, too. But don't cry, Mary. I didn't mean to be cross. Run out, like a good girl, and make it up with Twok before dinner. I know you didn't mean to hurt her, and I'm sure she will never offend in that way again if you tell her you are sorry."

Mary went out to find Twok, but came back in a few minutes to say that the child was nowhere in sight.

Joy looked a little anxious, but said, "Well, let us sit down to dinner. She is not such a silly child as to run away from us all on account of that slap. She'll be very angry for a little while and then she'll come back as penitent as if she were entirely to blame. I haven't been studying that child's character for a year for nothing, I hope. She's going to make a fine woman, and I'm growing prouder of her every day. Just see if she doesn't come back in half-an-hour and tell you she's sorry, and that she will never do it again."

Mary ate her dinner in silence, almost choking over it sometimes as she thought how wrongly she had acted in striking Twok. Still she was not at all convinced that Joy was right. She was sure the minister knew what swearing was better than Joy did, although she thought Joy was very wise about some things.

CHAPTER VII.

LIKE many other Canadian towns and villages, Linklater received its name from its first settler. Paul Linklater was one of those upholders of British rule in America to whom the name of United Empire Loyalists has been applied ; a name almost of opprobrium in the United States, but one of honor in Canada. At the close of the war, partly from a desire to live under British rule and partly on account of the confiscation of his property, he removed to Upper Canada, where he obtained a large grant of land from the Government, built a rude house, began to cultivate a portion of his land and in time surrounded himself with all the necessaries and many of the luxuries of life. He was assisted in his operations by his only son Peter, to whom he left all his property at his death. Peter started a saw mill and a grist mill, and before long a thriving little village sprang up around the old homestead. Having acquired a fortune by the success of his mills and the sale of some of his lands, Peter Linklater built a large and handsome but somewhat old fashioned stone house on a high hill which overlooked Lake Ontario, and from which on a clear day Niagara might be seen with a small telescope. The front of the house looked toward the lake, and at the left hand at no great distance from the house was a deep ravine through which a rapid creek flowed, almost losing itself in a swamp before it reached Lake Ontario, about seven miles away. The stone for the house and out-buildings as well as for the mills, a church and a school house, was taken from a quarry in this ravine, and after the completion of the buildings the water of the creek was directed into the quarry, where it formed a deep pond, which was almost surrounded by steep banks of rock and sand. Shortly after his removal to the new house Peter Linklater's wife died, leaving one child, a boy called Charles. This boy was sent away to a New York school, and for years saw little of his father, who soon married again. Peter Linklater's second wife gave birth to a child of singular beauty, who mysteriously disappeared when quite young. When Charles was about twenty-two years of age his father and step-mother both died, and he came into possession of the property. He married a young lady of the village, who died a year and a half after their marriage, leaving him a little boy to care for. He seemed very much dispirited at the loss of his wife, and from this time forth had little communication with anyone except his farm servants and his little boy Alvin. The mills he sold. Early in life he had proposed to enter the ministry, but after spending a year in the study of theology and finding what he considered absurdities in the creeds of the different churches, he cast the whole system of theology aside and declared his disbelief in revealed religion and a personal God. Most boys are brought up to believe in some creed, and to look with more or less disapproval upon all other beliefs. Alvin Linklater was taught to regard all creeds as false and absurd. The boy had few companions, but his father was very fond of him and endeavored to supply the place of mother and playmates. Alvin was never miserable and seldom lonely, but he was never very happy, for much of the joy and gladness of life must be lost to the boy who has no mother, no playmates and, worst of all, no belief in God. Alvin had great respect for his father and did not doubt that he was right, but sometimes he wished that he were wrong. His favorite place of resort when alone was the foot of an old elm tree, which grew on a bank that almost overhung the quarry. Here he would read the few story books he had, works on history and science, and the Bible; for although the father disbelieved in the inspiration of the Bible, he recognized its great literary merits, and thought it would do the boy no harm to read it. So Alvin often read the venerable book beneath the shade of the old elm. He would grow indignant over the deceptive meanness of Jacob, the wickedness of Jacob's sons and the cruel massacre of helpless women and children by the Jews, and shudder to think how anyone could believe in a God who would sanction and direct such atrocities. But when he came to the New Testament and read of Jesus, his kindness, compassion and universal love, he said to himself, "What a pity it isn't true!"

There was another person besides his father who took a great interest in Alvin and tried to fill the place of a mother. This was Mrs. Gerty, his father's house-keeper, an old woman who had lived with the family as a servant when a girl, had left it to get married and returned to it when her husband died. Mrs. Gerty often entertained the boy with stories of her early experiences. There was a store-room in the house in which old books, old clothes, and lumber of all kinds were stowed away. Mrs. Gerty always intended to clear this room and dispose of the rubbish, but somehow never found time to do so. When Alvin was about fourteen years old, he went to this room one day to look for an old book which his father had mentioned. He could not find the book, but his attention was drawn to a girl's broad brimmed hat of the finest straw which hung on a peg on the wall. He took this down, wondering who had worn it and determined to ask Mrs. Gerty to whom it belonged. Accordingly after tea he went to the kitchen, where Mrs. Gerty was making pies, and asked to whom the hat belonged.

"Did you never hear about it?"

"No."

"Well, that hat knows something that nobody else knows," said Mrs. Gerty, impressively, speaking of the hat as if it were a person.

"Tell me about it," said Alvin.

"Well, well, if you knew all, you wouldn't be so fond of sitting under that wicked old elm."

"Why?"

"Well, well, I'll begin at the beginning. Well, after your father's mother died, your grandfather married again, and his second wife presented him with the loveliest child that ever lived in this wicked world. You know I never exaggerate or flatter. I've often told you that you were not nearly so good looking as your father or any of the old Linklaters, so you will believe me when I say that none of the Linklaters could be compared with her. Oh, she was too good for this earth. Well, well, just wait until I dry my eyes. I can't talk with these tears. When Nellie was about nine years old she disappeared one day, leaving no trace behind her except that very hat which you have in your hand. It was too large for her head and must have fallen off when she went up."

"Went up?"

"Yes, some people thought she was drowned, but no trace of the body was found. Others said some wild animal must have taken her; but I always believed that she was translated like Elijah, for she was too good and too beautiful for this world."

Alvin did not believe in the story of Elijah, so he looked incredulous but said nothing.

"There is no reason," said Mrs. Gerty, "why a good person should not be translated now-a-days as well as in Bible times."

"Did they search the ravine?"

"Yes, and there is something strange about that which no one living in Linklater except me knows."

"What is that?"

"The creek in the ravine didn't always run as it does now into the quarry. There was a time when it flowed underground for quite a distance, disappearing suddenly into a hole and issuing again in a foaming torrent farther down the ravine. When Nellie was lost her father, after searching everywhere else, made up his mind that she had fallen into the stream and been carried underground. He at once set all his employes to work cutting a new channel for the stream, and toiled constantly at it himself until it was finished. Then they descended into the hole with lanterns and explored the bed of the stream, but were unable to find any trace of the body. When the search was over your grandfather had the holes closed up, for fear some one would fall in."

"I'd like to go down. Where were the holes?"

"I can't say. I never went into the ravine in those days, for it was a wild place then."

Alvin took the hat to his room and hung it on the wall in front of his bed, and then undressing went to bed, but lay awake, turning Mrs. Gerty's story over in his mind again and again. It was a bright moonlight night and his room, which had two large windows, was almost as light as day. The windows opened on a verandah, at one end of which was a tall poplar tree. It was very easy to descend from the verandah to the ground by means of this tree, and almost as easy to climb up again. Unable to sleep he dressed himself, and for want of another hat put on the one which he had found in the lumber room. The hat which was too large for the head of the aunt fitted snugly on that of the nephew. Walking along the verandah to the poplar tree, he made his way by means of it to the ground, and was soon running down a path toward the old elm. Sitting down under its spreading branches he watched the moon and the clouds, which were constantly changing shape, sometimes taking the semblance of one thing, sometimes of another. As the boy watched the sky he became drowsy, and before long fell fast asleep with his head against the tree; and as he slept he dreamed. His dream took the form of a vision, for he himself had no active part in it, but seemed to be merely a spectator. He saw a little girl sitting under the old elm, putting dandelions in the hat he had that day found. Her face was very lovely, and as she filled her hat with the yellow flowers she sang a song in a sweet voice. As he watched the child's face a strange feeling of dread came over him, and it seemed to him that he was not the only person who was looking at her. And then he saw, dimly at first, but afterward quite distinctly, a very handsome young man, with dark wavy hair and brown eyes, looking intently at the child. Alvin's attention was again drawn to the child, who looked around uneasily as if conscious that someone was watching her. The next moment the young man sprang forward, clasped the child in his arms and was gone. Alvin awoke in a great fright. He was very cold and was trembling from head to foot. Looking around he could see nothing but the trees, with their leaves rustling in the moonlight. Returning to the house, he climbed with more difficulty than usual to the verandah, and then looking back toward the old elm thought he saw a man standing under it, but looking again and seeing nothing concluded that he had been mistaken. He went to bed, but did not sleep until almost daylight. When he awoke the morning was well spent. Mrs. Gerty got breakfast for him, grumbling the while at the lateness of the hour.

"Was there anything in my aunt's hat when it was found?" he asked as he sat down at the table.

"Yes, it was full of dandelions."

"I thought you said it must have fallen off when she went up. How could she have it on, if it was full of dandelions?"

"Oh, I was forgetting about the dandelions. She could not have had it on, of course."

Alvin said no more, but he thought about it for weeks, and the more he thought the surer he felt that his dream was a faithful representation of what had really happened. He feared that his father would laugh at his superstition if he told him, and although he knew Mrs. Gerty would readily believe in his dream, he did not care to confide in her, knowing that she could not give him a sensible opinion. He searched the ravine carefully for some trace of the old channel of the stream, but could not find it ; and when he mentioned the matter to his father, Mr. Linklater said,

"That is probably one of Mrs. Gerty's stories. Of course I was away from home much of the time and the ravine was a wild place then, into which few people went; but I surely would have heard something of it if the stream had ever run underground."

One day while Alvin was walking in the garden he saw a child sitting under the elm, and stationed himself behind a tree to watch her. Her figure reminded him very strongly of the child in his dream, and when she turned her head he thought the face very like, too, although it did not seem quite the same and she was dressed quite differently, but as she sat there with her hat in her lap, she reminded him so strongly of his dream that he almost expected to see it enacted over again. In a few moments she tripped away, and climbing over the fence passed down the road. His mind was somewhat disturbed by the incident, and in order to compose it somewhat he took his fishing rod and went down to the ravine. The fish did not bite that afternoon, and after waiting patiently for half an hour he walked farther up the stream in the hope of meeting with greater success. Having walked for some distance up stream he noticed a path which led through the woods away from the creek. Wondering where this led to, he followed it, but had not gone far before he saw a large, savage-looking dog in front of him. Alvin was not a coward, but not liking the looks of the dog he concluded to go back. The dog started after him and then Alvin did a very foolish thing : he began to run. Now this dog was not at all ill-natured, but when Alvin ran he felt in duty bound to chase him. Alvin ran on, stumbling over the trees, tearing his clothes on the bushes and at last falling into a pool of water. Then, finding that the dog had given up the chase and that his clothes were torn and wet and covered with mud, he was much ashamed of himself, and thought he had better start for home. But in which direction should he start? He had lost the path. He would climb a tree to see where he was. Selecting a tree which looked easy to climb, he was soon at the top, and having descried a number of familiar objects and noted the direction in which he should proceed, began to descend. It was more difficult to climb down than to climb up, and as he was clinging to one of the branches while feeling for a foothold, it suddenly snapped off and he fell to the ground. Stunned by the fall, he lay there unconscious for some time. Then coming to his senses, he tried to rise but was unable to do so, on account of a severe pain in his right leg and shoulders. He must lie there, he thought, until someone found him. But would anyone ever find him? He might starve to death before anyone came, for he lay concealed in a wood at some distance from home. Weak from loss of blood, for he had cut his head in falling, he grew very faint and soon became unconscious again. When he next opened his eyes and looked up half unconsciously, he saw with no surprise whatever this time a pretty little girl, with blue eyes and a wonderfully sweet mouth that was quivering with pity. It was the child he had seen under the elm. She kneeled beside him on the grass and said,

"Poor boy! I wonder is he dead!"

Alvin said nothing, but looked at her; and she, somewhat relieved to see his eyes open, took out her handkerchief and bound it around his head in a way that would have done credit to a surgeon.

"Are you a real girl," said Alvin at last, "or are you only a dream?"

The child pinched her face and gave a stray lock of hair a very hard pull to convince herself that she was a real girl before speaking. Then she said,

"There have been so many strange things in my life that I often think myself that it is all a dream, but really I don't believe that I am a dream girl."

"Are you my aunt?"

"Why, how silly! How could a little girl like me be aunt to a big boy like you? I am only Twok. But your head is bleeding again. Have you a knife?"

Alvin tried to put his hand in his pocket, but his shoulder pained so that he could not do it. Twok put her hand in his pocket and took out his knife. Then, while he looked on wonderingly, she cut off the skirt of her dress and, kneeling down again in her petticoat, bound the dress skillfully about his head.

"The handkerchief wasn't big enough," she said in explanation. "Could you try to walk now?"

Alvin did try to raise himself, but without success.

"If Joy were only here. He is so strong and he knows everything."

"Why, do you know Joy Cougles?"

"Yes, of course. He is my brother now," said Twok, with no little pride in her voice.

Alvin had not talked to Joy for more than a year, although he occasionally met him, and as he did not often go to the village he had heard nothing of Twok's arrival. He thought it was queer that he never heard before that Joy had a sister.

"I will have to go away and get somebody," said Twok.

"I wish you wouldn't leave me," said Alvin. "Wouldn't somebody come for us soon?"

"You're not afraid to stay alone, are you?" said she in a somewhat contemptuous tone.

"No, but it seems so much nicer when you are here that I don't mind the pain so much. If we are both missing they will surely hunt for us, and may find us here."

"But *may* won't do. It is *must*. Your head is badly cut. Your leg may be broken, and you will be so stiff before long that they can't move you. I know the way all right and won't be long gone."

So saying Twok ran away with all speed. It so happened that the nearest house was that of Dr. Somerville, and when the child met him at the door he heard her story with interest, and bringing some bandages from the house accompanied her, leaving directions for his assistant to follow with a wagon. Alvin endured the pain bravely until Twok returned with the doctor, who examined his head, leg and shoulder, and looked rather grave. The leg was broken a little above the ankle and the shoulder was sprained. The doctor with the help of his assistant set the broken limb and moved him to the wagon, which was full of cushions. Then directing his assistant to see the boy safely home and promising to follow shortly himself, he told Twok that he would drive her home in his carriage.

"And you are Joy Cougles' little girl, are you?" he said.

"Yes," she said, "I'm Twok."

"Well, you're a very pretty little girl, and a good one too. But what are you going to do for a dress?"

"Twok looked down in dismay at her petticoat and the tears came into her eyes. The doctor stooped down and wiped the tears away very tenderly as he said,

"Never mind your dress, Twok. You shall have a prettier one."

They had reached the house, and he was soon consulting with his wife, a stout motherly-looking woman, who hugged Twok and kissed her and hugged her again, until she was almost crushed. Then she went up-stairs and came down again with a very pretty dress, and said with tears in her eyes,

"It belonged to my little Millie, who is dead. You shall have it, and you must come and see us sometimes with it on."

Twok kissed her in sympathy and submitted to another hugging while the doctor turned away his head, wiped his eyes, and said he had an infernal cold. Mrs. Somerville put the dress on Twok and kissed her good bye, and the doctor having lifted her into his carriage drove away toward the village.

"I'm going to take you home first," said he, "and then

I'll take another look at that boy. What are Joy and his mother teaching you?"

"Everything."

"Then I suppose you are very wise?"

"Oh, no. Not yet, but I will be."

"And can you read?"

"Oh, yes. Joy says he never saw anyone learn so quickly. He did really."

"And I suppose he taught you in the same old way. Now if you were my little girl—and, by Jingo, I wish you were—you should learn to read in the way that will be universally adopted before you are an old woman. As it is, you will have to unlearn what you are learning now when you are grown up."

"How would you teach me?"

"Oh, I can't tell you now. Here you are at home. You will have to come and see me some day, and I will explain to you my hobby."

She jumped into Joy's arms and the doctor drove off, saying to Joy,

"She'll tell you all about it. I'm in a hurry."

CHAPTER VII.

"WHY, where have you been, Twok?" said Joy, as he carried the little girl into the house. Then Twok told her story. She had never been struck before since leaving old Meg, and when Mary slapped her face she was very angry. She did not even know that the obnoxious word 'damn' had slipped out, and could not imagine why Mary had slapped her. She walked along the road for a little way, feeling very naughty. Then she remembered that God was looking at her and that He could feel the anger at her heart as well as she could. So she said, "Please make me good." It was only her heart that said it; the lips did not move, but it was wonderful how differently she felt afterwards. She was about to return and ask Mary to forgive her and tell her what she had done that was wrong, when she remembered that Mary loved flowers. She had obtained permission to go to the ravine immediately after dinner. She was not hungry, and why should she not go without her dinner and get Mary some flowers as a peace offering? On the way she saw the hill on which Broadglance, as the Linklater residence was called, was situated, and thinking she might be able to see Hamilton from it, climbed over the fence and made her way to the old elm, where she remained a few moments before going to the ravine. In the ravine she found Alvin Linklater.

Joy told Twok why Mary had slapped her, and then said, "'Damn' is a word which little girls shouldn't use. It's a good word in the right place, but a very poor word in the wrong place, and as you are very apt to use it in the wrong place, you must not use it at all."

"Oh, Twok, I'm so sorry I slapped you," said Mary, "but you really were very naughty."

"I didn't mean to say it," said Twok, "and I will try very hard never to say it again. I had such a nice bouquet of flowers for you, but I left it in the woods. I'll have to give you a kiss instead."

Twok did not know the name of the boy whom she found in the woods, but Joy learned from the doctor that it was Alvin Linklater, and called to see him several times. Alvin more than once commenced to tell Joy about his dream, but always changed his mind. At last one day about three weeks after the accident he said to Joy,

"Do you believe in dreams?"

"Well, after a fashion. I have some ideas of my own about dreams. Have you been dreaming?"

Alvin told his dream. He had already learned from Joy how Twok came to him, and now, after telling the dream he said,

"How do you account for Twok being so like the child of my dream?"

"A good deal of imagination, I suspect. All the surroundings would tend to remind you of the dream and you would very easily get the two faces, the dream one and the reality, mixed. Her hair and eyes might be the same. There would be nothing remarkable in that. I can conceive it possible that your dream might be a fairly faithful representation of what really occured, but I cannot believe that my little girl has any connection with it. Your aunt disappeared many years ago and would be a woman if she were still alive. But Alvin, you must promise me never to say anything to Twok about that dream. She would think so much about it with her clever little brain that she might go crazy over it."

"I promise. Let her come and see me and I won't say a word about that."

"It would excite you too much. That was a pretty bad

cut on your head and you look pale yet. You must not think of that dream. I have no doubt that it was a mere coincidence that you dreamed of dandelions in the hat. But the doctor has invited Twok to go for a drive with him to-morrow. I will tell him that you wish to see her and perhaps he will bring her to you. But it is time I was home."

With that he took his leave. A few hours afterward Dr. Somerville called at the shop of the young blacksmith, and Joy told him of Alvin's dream.

"You don't think it could mean anything, do you?" said the doctor.

"Well, I don't know. It might possibly, although I wouldn't tell him so. I have thought a great deal about dreams lately, and if you like will read you a short essay which I have written in my note-book."

"Do, Joy."

Joy took out his note-book and read:

"THE WILL AND THE BRAIN.

"As man was made in the image of God, and God is a spirit—man must also be a spirit, acting through his material body. The external, material body cannot be regarded as the man himself. It is only a machine with which he works and through which only he can now operate. Each part of this machine is specially adapted to certain purposes. When a man wishes to go to any place, he is obliged to employ means to accomplish his purpose, and usually makes use of his legs; when he wishes to solve a mathematical problem, he must utilize his brain. The brain may be said to have two functions: it is the medium through which man thinks and it may also be regarded as the telegraph office where the will transmits its orders through the nerves to the different parts of the body. It has been held that the brain cannot be regarded as an instrument, as it appears to act of its own accord; but, under ordinary circumstances, the action of other parts of the body seems also spontaneous. A man usually exercises no thought about the movement of his legs in walking and is hardly conscious of the operation of his will. When the legs through weariness do not readily perform the duty required and answer to the commands of will, then there is conscious action of the will. We force motion with an effort. The brain like the legs usually seems to be working by itself, and it is only when some line of thought beyond its ordinary capacity is required that we are conscious of any separate and distinct action of the will. When we wish to make an abstruse calculation which requires deep thought, we are conscious of a working of the will upon the brain; we are conscious of collecting our thoughts and bringing all the forces of the brain to bear upon the solution of the question; we are conscious of a determination to shut out all other thoughts and concentrate all the powers of the brain upon that one point. The body, like other machines, is subject to waste, and is always being renewed by fresh supplies of food and oxygen, and by a wise provision of nature man is not allowed to use it constantly, for otherwise, having little chance for recuperation, it would be quickly worn out like any other overworked machine. But at regular intervals the will loses control of the body, and what we call sleep occurs. One of the functions of the brain is then usually entirely suspended; for the will, having lost control of the brain, cannot telegraph commands to the different parts of the body, which consequently have a time of rest, when the tissues have an opportunity for regeneration. The brain, freed from the control of will, still acts in a desultory, ineffective way in what we call dreams, but as there is no guiding influence, these dreams, these random actions of the brain, are usually absurd and nonsensical. In conversation we pass from one subject to another, touching upon many different topics and perhaps concluding with one having no apparent connection with the subject that first engaged the attention; yet it is often easy to trace the connection between the various ideas leading to such a result. It is only by an effort, as a rule, that we can keep the mind fixed on one subject, so powerful is the suggestiveness of ideas. This is during waking hours. But when we sleep, the will, having no control of the brain, exerts no check upon these ideas, and so they follow each other swiftly, a dream requiring hours for its actual accomplishment being begun and terminated in a few seconds. When awake there is the same tendency to the rapid association of ideas, but the powers of reflection being active cause us to linger upon each idea; and moreover the numerous objects of outward sense are always making some impression upon the brain, and we are always making comparisons between our ideas and the realities with which we are surrounded or which we have some time experienced; whereas in sleep there are no realities, no external objects opposing themselves to the fantasies of the brain, and consequently there is a wider scope for the various concatinations of ideas. While we are awake reason holds the reins, and the will exerts an influence upon the many images that impress themselves upon the brain and the multitudinous associations connected therewith; arresting them in their course, breaking their connection, changing their direction, contrasting them with each other and dismissing them at pleasure. But when we sleep the various images, uninfluenced and undirected by the will, follow each other in rapid succession according to unknown laws of association and suggestion. During our waking existence a sensation of pain affecting any part of the body, as when the hand comes in contact with fire, is telegraphed to the brain by the nerves, and the will at once sends an order to remove the hand from the fire. In sleep any violent sensation causes the will to reassume its control of the brain, or in other words awakes the sleeper; but an ordinary sensation may have no effect upon the will and yet make an impression upon the brain, giving rise to certain associations of ideas. Although there is no volition in complete sleep, the brain occasionally hits upon the solution of a mathematical problem or a poetical stanza, but such cases are so exceptional that they only serve by the contrast to show the ordinary inefficiency of the organ without the controlling influence of will. When the body is in its normal condition the brain, acting by itself, has no control over it; but we occasionally meet with cases where the body answers to the fancies of the brain and moves in response—such is the case with somnambulists who walk, ride and climb in their sleep, going into places of great danger which they would avoid when awake. When the brain is freed from the control of will, it may be more susceptible to other influences; and although dreams are usually the random actions of an unguided machine called the brain, it seems as if an outside power sometimes takes control. The prophetical dreams might be accounted for by supposing that, when a man loses control of his brain in sleep, God sometimes impresses images upon it and directs the flow of ideas. It would appear that mind acts upon mind perhaps in accordance with some law of attraction, so that the thoughts of one person are sometimes impressed upon the brain of another without any apparent communication between them. It often happens that companions think of the same thing at the same moment, and there are persons gifted with the faculty of mind reading. Now as the brain, which is merely a mass of grey and white nervous matter composed of water, fat, albumen and certain salts, can receive impressions, retain images and generate ideas, some other forms of matter may possess the same quality in a lesser degree; it may also be that when the brain is uncontrolled by the will it becomes susceptible to the influence of the impressions made on these forms of matter, and this would account for much of the phenomena of spiritualism as well as for some of our dreams. As there is a state when we are wide awake —that is, when the will has complete control of the body— and a state when we are fast asleep, the will having lost all control of the body, so there is a state when the will has partial control and there is a certain degree of consciousness: we have a dim perception of the objects surrounding us and mingle them with our dreams, so that when we awake we are not certain whether it was a dream or a reality. Objects of outward sense seem then to impress themselves upon the brain and form images there, but the will does not in any way influence the course of the ideas to which they give rise, although with an effort it might then assert its control.

Joy finished reading, and, closing his note-book, said,
"Now, I do not think that either the old elm or Alvin's aunt's hat can have any consciousness of what happened years ago, but still it might possibly have been impressed upon them in some way just as it would be impressed on a brain, and if there were any such impressions there his brain was just in the proper condition to receive them. He had heard Mrs. Gerty's story. His aunt's hat was on his head and his head was resting against the tree, while he was fast asleep."

"Why, if you are right, Joy, it may be true enough that even the walls have ears. But are those all your own ideas?"

"Mostly all. Of course I have read books on such questions and have absorbed some ideas from them, moulding them again in my own brain and fitting them into others, but most of them are entirely original. I do not mean by that that no one has ever thought of them before. I have often struck a bright idea and thought for months that no one had ever thought of that before, and then some day I would read a book that I had never opened before and find the same idea expressed there in a much better way than I could express it."

CHAPTER IX.

THE doctor thought Twok would be very good medicine for Alvin, and took her to see him, with the understanding that she would go home with him to stay all night when he called for her.

When Twok entered Alvin's room and saw him sitting in an easy chair by the window, she went forward and shook hands with him.

"Bring that rocking chair and sit near me," he said. "I wish I were strong enough to bring it for you myself."

Twok brought the chair, sat down, and after a few moments of silence said,

"Do you think it was God that caused you to fall down and get hurt?"

"Why?" said Alvin, hoping to gain time, for he somehow didn't like to tell this little girl that he didn't believe in God.

"Mary said it was God that caused it, and she thought it was intended to punish you or teach you a lesson; but Joy said God had nothing to do with it. He believed that it was all your own fault, and said God would be above throwing a boy out of a tree. What do you think yourself?"

"Why, Twok, I don't believe in God."

"Don't you? Who do you think made the world?"

"Well, I don't know; but if God made the world, who made God? It is just as hard to suppose that God can exist without a creator, as to suppose that the world does. But there is no use asking a little girl like you such a question."

"No. I can't answer that out of my own mind, but I'll ask Joy to tell me. He knows almost everything. I'm sorry you don't believe in God, because you can't have anyone to pray to, and it makes me feel so happy to pray. When I'm naughty I just say down in my heart, 'Please make me good,' and then I feel so sorry that I was bad, and I'm quite happy again in a moment. One day I was quite naughty and knew I ought to pray to be good, but didn't want to be good then and I wouldn't pray for a long time. So I kept feeling naughtier and naughtier, until at last I thought, 'Suppose I should get so bad that God couldn't make me good.' Then I was frightened and prayed right off, and the naughty feeling all went away."

"Would you like to come and play with me when I get well? I'll show you all over the place and let you ride on my horse. Would you like that?"

"Why, yes. But I won't promise to come until I hear what Joy and his mother say. They will know best. Can you ride fast?"

"Well, the horse I have now doesn't go very fast. You see the one I had before threw me one day, so my father sold it and bought this one, which doesn't run so fast, but is very gentle. It will be very nice for you to ride on."

"If I were a boy," said Twok, "I wouldn't let a horse throw me. I would hold on tight and make him be quiet," and she stamped her little foot on the floor as if to show how she would stamp the viciousness out of a horse.

"I wouldn't fall out of a tree either," she continued.

"I see you don't think much of me," said Alvin, looking much disconcerted.

"Oh, I'm so sorry," said Twok, "I didn't mean to say anything to hurt you. Will you please to forgive me?"

"Forgive you? Why there isn't anything to forgive. I'm only too glad to have such a pretty little girl come to see me."

"Do you really think I'm very pretty?"

"Awfully pretty. Go look at yourself in the glass."

Twok turned to look at the mirror, rather for the purpose

of inspecting it than herself, for she had never before seen such a handsome looking-glass. As she did so Dr. Somerville opened the door and looked in.

"I think you have had your share of this little angel, Alvin," said he, "and now I'm going to take her home with me."

"Am I as pretty as an angel?" said Twok, turning to the doctor.

"Why, you conceited little thing. What makes you think that?"

"What did you call me an angel for, then?"

"Well, by Jingo, if angels are any prettier than you are, I wish I may die to-morrow and go to live with them. But you needn't get conceited about it. 'Handsome is as handsome does,' and pretty girls are sometimes not half so nice as plain ones. They get to think so much of themselves. Besides pretty girls don't always make pretty women, and the very prettiest of young women sometimes make very disagreeable old women. Now, if I had a little girl I would far rather have her not at all pretty at first, but grow into a good-looking, sweet tempered old woman, than to have her start off as pretty as you are and end up a discontented, sour-mouthed, unhappy old woman, as lots of pretty girls do. When you are very young your face is as God makes it, but when you are old it is as you make it yourself. If you are very good and pure and unselfish, you will have a lovely face when you grow old; but if you are selfish and discontented and quarrelsome your face will begin to look like yourself. But you won't make a lovely face by looking often in the glass. The way to do it is to be good and to do good. The face you have when you are old will be the one you will go to heaven with. Now, I would rather come into the world with a homely face and go to heaven with a lovely one, than come into the world with a pretty face and go out of it with an ugly one. Wouldn't you, Twok?"

"Why, yes," said Twok; "because you have to live longer in heaven than you do in the world."

They said good-bye to Alvin and drove off to Dr. Somerville's house, where Twok was received with a great deal of hugging and kissing, and not a few tears by Mrs. Somerville. After tea was over, Twok said to the doctor,

"Now will you tell me about your hobby?"

"My hobby! Ha, ha! So you want to know about my hobby, do you? Who told you I had a hobby?"

"You did yourself. You said, 'Come and see me and I'll tell you all about my hobby.'"

"Well, so I will, some day when you are older. I'm afraid you are too young to understand it now."

"If I'm too young to understand it, it can't be a very good way to teach little children to read."

"To be sure, to be sure. But then it may be much more difficult to teach you why it is the best way than it would be to teach the thing itself. If the system were adopted, it wouldn't be necessary to tell the children why it was the best system. No, you must wait."

When it was bedtime Mrs. Somerville took the child upstairs, and when she was ready for bed said,

"Now say your prayers to me, dear."

"I never say prayers to anyone but God," replied Twok as she kneeled down by the bed, and Mrs. Somerville stood by and wept because she remembered how her own little girl prayed at bedtime, and then the poor mother tucked the child snugly in bed, kissed her good-night and went down stairs to ask her husband if he couldn't persuade Joy to give the child up to them.

"I wouldn't be mean enough to ask him," growled the doctor.

"But never mind, perhaps our little Millie is loving us and planning for us in heaven better than she could here."

It was some months before Twok heard anything more of the doctor's hobby, but one day when he called to see Joy the young blacksmith said,

"Twok says you know an easy way to teach children to read. How would you do it?"

"How do you pronounce the word c-o-l-o-n-e-l?" said the doctor.

"Kurnel," responded Joy.

"That's right and yet it isn't right. That isn't the way it looks. Now some fools want to change the spelling of the word to make it accord with the pronunciation. They would spoil all our best libraries and compel us to buy everything new for the sake of making spelling accord with pronunciation. They would make us forget all the old derivations and so destroy half our understanding of the language. And then, after going to the expense of printing all the old books over with the new spelling and teaching everybody a new system, they would have to begin all over again, for the pronunciation of words is always changing. Now what I propose is this: Instead of changing the spelling of words to suit the pronunciation I would change the pronunciation to make it accord with the spelling. You could not have done that five hundred years ago, because so few of the people could read, and they went right on mispronouncing words until they changed the whole face of the language. The scholars, who knew how to pronounce the words rightly, had to pronounce them wrongly too, so the people could understand them. For a long time the scholars kept changing the spelling to make it accord with the changing pronunciation or mispronunciation, but at last there were so many books that they fixed a standard of spelling. So now we have two languages—the spoken language and the written one. Take the word 'colonel.' It is spelled the way it was once pronounced and the way it ought to be pronounced now. There are hundreds of other words that we mispronounce every day in the same way, and if it were not for the fact that everybody reads so much in these days we would pronounce them still more wrongly. That is the real secret of the confusion of tongues. Reading keeps the tendency to mispronunciation in check. If it were not for that, we would already have so changed the English language in Canada that Englishmen could not understand us. But the fact is it is more generally pronounced correctly in Canada than in England, because everybody reads here. We have no literary class, but we have the best common schools of the world. You will find people in adjoining counties of England speaking different dialects—that is, each section has its own peculiar way of mispronouncing English; but throughout this great broad country, where we might sink England in the great lakes and never miss it, we all speak very much the same dialect of English."

"That is a new idea to me," said Joy; "I suppose that is why there are so many dialects in Greek."

"Yes," said Dr. Somerville. "The common people of Greece had the same bad habit of mispronouncing their language as the common people of England, and the scholars tried to follow them. Different districts had different dialects. Now the student of Greek has to master all these dialectic peculiarities, all these mispronunciations. If my scheme were adopted, it would not only be the means of keeping the variations of pronunciation still more in check, but it would make it very easy to learn to read all languages. Suppose all civilized nations would agree to pronounce words according to the way they are spelled. Why, they could appoint a commission to frame simple rules for pronunciation that would apply to all languages. If I wish to study French, the great difficulty in my way is that I don't know how to pronounce the words. I could master the vocabulary and the grammar of the language in a short time, if I were not bothered with the pronunciation. I do not suppose it would be possible to carry so great a scheme as that, but I do not see why the literary men of English speaking countries could not by a combined effort bring about a general reform in pronunciation in this age of general reading. It would probably be necessary to change the spelling of a few words in the first place, but once establish a system of pronunciation and our language would remain the same for ages, except that we would always be adding new names to represent new discoveries. Words would of course sometimes undergo changes of meaning, but the tendency to that is already held in check by reading. If the system I propose were adopted, we would still have the advantage of knowing the derivations of words, and our old authors would not be mutilated; while instead of children wasting time in learning to spell, they would only have to read, and how much reading they would be able to do with the extra time at their disposal!"

Twok had been standing by, listening, with wide open eyes, and now the doctor turning to her said,

"Well, Twok, you have heard the old man's hobby explained. Do you understand it?"

"I think I partly know what you mean," said Twok, "but often when you were talking I couldn't understand at all. I guess you will have to tell me all over again when I grow older."

CHAPTER X.

OF the people of Linklater Twok knew very little. She was scarcely more familiar with the children of the village than she had been with those who lived in the vicinity of Meg's Rest. This was not because any restraint was placed upon her actions by Joy and his mother. She was allowed to roam at will when not engaged in little duties about the house, or in studying the lessons set by the young blacksmith, but she always chose to wander by herself. She loved the woods, and would often clamber down one of the steep paths leading to the ravine, sometimes stopping on the way to grasp the low hanging branches of the trees, and swing on them till her arms were tired. Then reaching the bottom of the ravine she would stroll among the trees, gathering wild flowers, or wade in the creek that tumbled over the rocks, now looking into the watery mirror and wondering whether the fishes could see the reflection of her face there, now trying to catch the fish in her hands, but always replacing them carefully in the water after examining them. Twok's fondness for the water grew out of a story of a water nymph, in which she was greatly interested. She knew that the story was imaginary, but it took her fancy so, that water had a new charm for her. Gazing into the brook one day, her mind full of stories of nymphs and fairies, she saw the reflection of her face there for the first time and thought she had discovered a real nymph in the water. Then noticing that the nymph looked like herself and comparing the reflection with the one she had often seen in the looking glass, she exclaimed after a moment's consideration,

"Why, it is only looking-water!"

After that she was always playing in the water, and that is the way she got acquainted with the fishes, of which she became so fond that she refused to eat them at the table, and would put her hands over her eyes when she met boys returning from a day's fishing carrying strings loaded with the finny creatures.

There was one part of the ravine that was always avoided by the villagers. In a hollow just below the quarry pond stood the ruins of an old stone mill, and not far from the mill was the miller's log house, built close against a rocky bank. The mill had been burned many years before, and the miller, who perished in the flames, was said to haunt the ruins. The house was unoccupied after the miller's death until an old man named Carlock called on Mr. Linklater one day and offered to buy the place. Mr. Linklater would not sell it, but told Carlock that he could have undisputed possession of the house, so long as he paid a nominal rent, to which the old man readily agreed and at once took possession. What he did for a living no one knew, but he was generally regarded as crazy.

In one of her expeditions Twok came upon Carlock's house. She had heard the place described, but the villagers said no one except Carlock ever entered it. She had often met the old man on the road and he had always seemed pleased when she smiled and bowed. She would call on him and see what his house was like. Old Carlock answered her rap, with a fierce look on his face, but when he saw who it was his expression changed wonderfully, and when she said,

"I have come to see you, Mr. Carlock," he said,

"Come in."

She entered a very ordinary looking cabin, with no floor but that which nature made, no furniture except a bedstead, a large cupboard, one chair, which he gave her, and a rickety old table that looked to Twok as if it would fall over if a cup of water were placed on it; and that reminded her that she wanted a drink of water, so she said sweetly,

"I am so thirsty. Could you give me a drink of water?"

The old man did not answer. He seemed to have forgotten her presence, and stood looking abstractedly at the cupboard.

"She will not reveal my secret," he said to himself. "My hobby will be safe with her."

Twok forgot all about her thirst. How strange that she should know two men with hobbies. Opening the door of the cupboard, Carlock touched a spring at the bottom with his foot, and a trap door flew open. He beckoned her to follow him and began to descend. After a moment's hesitation, curiosity overcame fear, and entering the cupboard she looked down. A ladder leaned against the wall, below the door, and Twok could touch the top rung with her foot. Carlock who now stood at the bottom, about five feet below, said,

"Don't be afraid. I'll catch you if you fall."

She carefully descended, and in a moment stood in a passage that seemed to lead into the side of the hill against which the cabin was built. This passage was much lighter than the cabin, and looking to see where the light came from, Twok noticed a small jet of gas burning.

"Where does the flame come from?" she asked.

"It is natural gas," he said. "The hills are full of it for miles around in every direction."

They had come to the end of the passage, and Carlock opening another door they entered a brilliantly lighted room.

"I found a hole here," he said, "and thought it might be a cave. It turned out to be a very small affair, hardly big enough to turn around in, but I enlarged it myself. I think it must have been at one time the bed of a stream. It extends for some distance back, but I only occupy this end, which I have closed off from the rest. The gas was burning when I found it, and air came in through a crevice. The roof was of rock and so low that I could hardly stand up straight, but the sides and floor were of clay, and I had nothing to do but use my pick and shovel to lower the floor and enlarge the room. It took me a long time to complete the work, especially to provide for ventilation; but I've got things into pretty good shape now. I made all the furniture myself, too. That big window up there closes my den off from the rest of the cave. That is where the water must have flowed through when the stream ran here."

Twok looked around the room. The furniture consisted of a bed, a table, two easy chairs, a very large cupboard, two enormous blue boxes, and, what surprised Twok most of all, a forge. He saw her look of surprise, and said,

"You are surprised. So would other people be if they knew my secret. You will never reveal it?"

"Never!"

"I make knives, child—the best that are made in America. They are stamped with the name of a well-known English firm, and are sold in Canada and the United States. The hardware men with whom I deal know good knives when they see them, and they do not ask too many questions when they have a chance to make a good bargain and save the duty besides. They are smuggled into the States, but I have nothing to do with that."

"Isn't it wicked to pretend that an English firm makes them? It seems like stealing their trade."

"You don't intend to betray me?" said Carlock fiercely.

"I said I wouldn't."

"There's no harm in it. What right have Englishmen to sell their goods in Canada? They have their own markets; why should they want ours? People talk of a protective tariff, but what we want is a prohibitive tariff, so high as to shut out foreign goods altogether. Suppose I mark my knives with my own name? Who would buy them? People don't test things for themselves. They go by the name, and they have an idea that a thing manufactured in Canada cannot be worth much. People always prefer things made far away from home, in a foreign country. Now if we had a prohibitive tariff for a few years, I would mark my knives with my own name and they would soon become famous. I have a way of using gas in finishing my knives that I won't explain even to you."

"Well, it doesn't seem right to me, and I'm sure Joy would not do it; but I promised I wouldn't tell, and I won't. Is that your hobby?"

"No, I don't exactly call this a hobby. My hobby is only partly a hobby. It has grown to be a sort of second nature with me now, but in the first place it was used chiefly as a cloak. I wanted people to think I was a queer old man with a hobby, so they wouldn't suspect what I was working at."

Twok wondered if it could be his hobby to be so very thin after having been so very fat, and to have his skin hang around his face so loosely that it made one wonder why he didn't have a piece cut out and sew it up again, to make it fit his face.

"I have made a hobby," he continued, "of collecting articles belonging to thieves, murderers and criminals, as well as those belonging to their victims."

Twok shuddered.

"It has cost me quite a bit, for I do it secretly, and very few people know anything about my hobby."

"You said you used it as a cloak."

"Yes, yes, I did start that way, but it's a real hobby now, and then I don't wish to court publicity. That might lead to detection. I keep myself to myself as much as possible, and very few people outside of Linklater have seen me except at night, and then I have been so disguised that you would not have recognized me. No, I don't publish my hobby, but if I should ever be discovered I can make use of it to blind people as to my real object in having this underground room and coming and going so strangely. Would you like to see my collection? I keep it in one of those big blue boxes."

Twok said "no" very quickly, and looked rather nervous.

"Perhaps you think I'm crazy, I talk so much. Well, I've been silent so long that after I have opened my mouth I feel like talking, even at the risk of discovery. It is human nature to want sympathy. It is the hardest thing in the world to keep a secret. Perhaps it is too much to ask you, but you have promised?"

"I never break my word."

"I know it. I see it in your face, and you were kind to me once. It is very kind to come and see me now. Why I might grow fat again if such a lively and pretty girl as you would come to live with me. I was very fat once, very fat."

Old Carlock laughed in such a good-humored way at the remembrance of it and looked so very different when he laughed, that his skin didn't seem to be such a bad fit after all, and Twok actually began to think that he was growing fat before her eyes. Then he lit the gas in a queer little stove which he told her he had made himself, and showing her a steel contrivance made especially for cooking meat over his gas stove, told her she might cook a piece of beef-steak for him and another for herself if she liked, but she must be sure and have his piece well done, very well done, or he couldn't eat it; and then he laughed so long and so heartily and seemed to be enjoying himself so vastly, that Twok was sure he was growing fat now, and looked at him with such interest that she forgot all about the meat and let it burn almost to a crisp. But old Carlock said that was just the way he liked it, and asked her if she would like to know what he was laughing at, and when she said that she was just aching to know, he told her that the children of Linklater were all sure that he never ate anything at all and that he encouraged them in this belief as much as possible; whereat Twok laughed, too, and seeing her laugh old Carlock laughed again with such violence this time that Twok became alarmed lest he might grow so very fat that his skin wouldn't hold him.

As Twok watched the old man, she noticed that he did not seem to need his staff there, and concluded that his weakness was in great part assumed. She was sure of this when after having eaten the meat which she had cooked, together with some bread, which she cut from a large loaf, he made her a knife, marked it with his own name and told her there was no deception in that, and it would do to remember him by. She thanked him for this and asked,

"Can I go home now?"

"Surely, surely," he said. "I am not an ogre to keep you here in my cave when you want to go. Don't come to see me often, please. I would like to have you come only folks might see you and wonder."

With that he led the way back to the cabin, and she felt a sense of relief as if a load had been lifted from her when, after saying good-bye, she stepped out doors and stood under the sky again. As she walked away she saw Sam Slemmings sneak out from behind a tree near the cabin, and that night she dreamed that she had the key of the big blue box in which Carlock kept his relics, and that Sam was chasing her in order to take it from her.

CHAPTER XI.

MRS. Cougles sat in her easy chair near the window one Sunday afternoon about three years after Twok's arrival in Linklater, with Twok on a low stool beside her, the child's head resting on the lap of the cripple, who stroked the golden hair with her hand as she said,

"What are you thinking of, my child?"

"I was thinking," said Twok raising her head, "how strange it is that, of all the millions of people in the world, no two look exactly alike, and that made me remember something that Dr. Somerville said one day."

"What was that?"

"He says that we make our own faces, and that if we are very good they will grow to look good at last, no matter how homely they were at first; but if we are bad they will grow to look like ourselves. The faces we have when we are very old are the ones we go to heaven with."

"Why, that is a pretty idea, Twok. I hope you will always remember it. Being good or being bad doesn't make much difference in the shape of the face, but it makes a wonderful difference in the expressions of the face. The expressions are indicative of character, and I think it is by them rather than by the features that we will know each other in heaven. Do you understand what I mean by character, Twok?"

"Yes, that is one of the things the hammer taught me. Character is the combination of qualities which distinguishes one person from another."

"Those are rather big words for so small a girl. Are you sure you know what they mean?"

"Oh, yes I do. Joy told me. He says man is his own maker, because he makes his own character. God thought it best to let man make himself."

"How about the little girls and the boys and the women?"

"Oh, Joy says man sometimes just means people, men or women, boys or girls, it doesn't make any difference."

"Did Joy tell you how to make character?"

"Why, yes. We can't make something out of nothing. We must have materials. Materials are what a thing is made of. The blacksmith's material is iron. Circumstances are the things out of which character is made."

"And what are circumstances?"

"The things that happen to us and the people we meet."

"But how can you tell what to do with the circumstances?"

"Joy says man is an animal with a conscience. The conscience tells what is right and what is wrong, and if you always do what it says you may make lots of mistakes, but they won't hurt your character."

"You have a good memory, Twok, and Joy ought to be proud of his pupil, but I don't think our characters depend altogether upon ourselves. The people with whom we associate have a great influence upon us. I know you are striving to grow to be a good woman. You must always remember that you are not only making your own character, but you are helping to make the characters of the people you meet. Every little thing you say or do affects your own character, and oftener than you imagine your actions will influence those of other people. But I wonder where Joy is. He seems to be taking a long walk, and Mary has not come yet either. It will soon be tea time."

"Here we are, mother," said Joy, entering with Mary, who, blushing in a most unaccountable way, came forward and, kneeling, laid her head where Twok's had been a few moments before. Mrs. Cougles bent over and kissed her as Joy said,

"She has promised to be my wife, mother. Will you take her as your daughter?"

"She has been a very good daughter to me for years, and I'm sure she will make a good wife for my boy. Kiss me, Joy."

Joy bent and kissed her, and then kneeled down beside Mary as Twok arose to leave the room, feeling that she was in the way.

"Don't go away, Twok," said Mrs. Cougles, putting one hand on the child's arm to detain her while she rested the other on Joy's head. "My family is growing rapidly. A little while ago I only had one boy. Now I have three children. But is it not time for tea? We cannot live on love alone."

"Let me get tea ready to-night," said Twok. But Mary insisted on doing the work as usual, and the girls went to the kitchen together.

"You will be my sister now, will you not?" said Twok, putting up her mouth for a kiss.

"Yes," said Mary stooping to kiss the upturned face.

Meanwhile Joy and his mother, left alone, sat in silence for some moments, the young man embarrassed in his mother's presence for the first time in his life; the heart of the woman too full for utterance. The silence was broken by a quick little sob that made Joy say in a startled voice,

"Mother!"

"Oh, my boy, my boy! Forgive me. I didn't mean to be so childish," she said, choking back another sob.

He lifted her in his arms tenderly, and sitting down in a chair held her close, while her slender frame shook with the effort to suppress the sobs.

"It will be all over in a moment, Joy," she said. "It is very foolish of me, but I had grown so accustomed to having you love me the best of all that I broke down for a minute."

"O my little mother, I do love you the best of all—far the best of all, still. It was very sudden. I was strolling in the ravine and found her crying there. That brute of a brother had been abusing her again. She looked so pretty and I felt so sorry for her, that I couldn't help it; but there is no hurry for marriage. I am twenty-one. She is eighteen. In five years I'll be twenty-six and she'll be twenty-three. We both think that will be soon enough."

"Tea is ready," said Twok, opening the door, and Joy carried his mother out to the dining-room.

"Twok has been reciting to me one of Joy's lectures on character," said Mrs. Cougles when they were seated.

"What is it?" asked Mary. "He never delivers any lectures to me."

"Because, when I do, you get tired of listening to me. I don't wish to bore you."

"Oh! I never said so, Joy."

"No, you are too kind to say so; but I can see that just when I am at the most important point of my argument, you are busily thinking of something else. Now, there are lots of things in which we are both interested, and so I talk to you of them. I'm afraid that if it were not for you I would get to be such a bore, always talking about my theories, that everybody would shun me."

"Well, give us your lecture on character now. You will have an audience of three and won't need to watch me to see if I understand it all."

"He says man makes himself," said Twok.

"Yes," said Joy. "Man is highly distinguished from all the other works of God by being allowed, by forming his own character, to create himself; for although, in so far as man's animal nature extends, he is entirely a created being, yet since the formation of character, which is the most important part of man, is greatly dependent upon his own actions, he may be said to be to some extent a self-created being. God does not create character, but he gives to each man a power of discerning between right and wrong and a free will to choose between them. It is the exercise of this will, together with the combination of outward circumstances and surroundings, that gives to man his character. Man comes into the world characterless, and it depends a great deal upon himself whether he shall develop into a noble being, or degrade into a mere animal. There is no limit to the time allotted to the formation of character, and consequently no limit to the perfection of character a man may attain to if he always makes the best possible use of all his opportunities. But although the formation of character is unending, the early stages of the process are perhaps the most important. There is nothing more difficult than the unmaking of character, and since it is in childhood that man's character begins to take shape, this must be considered the most important part of his life. Childhood measured by years is but a small portion of man's life, but is this measurement by years the true one in such a case? I have sometimes looked at the sky on a bright moonlight night when there were only a few clouds to be seen, and they were rapidly hurrying past the moon. It appeared as if the moon were rushing through the clouds when in reality they were passing over it, or between it and us, and I have thought that our estimate of time was something like this. Time is our way of looking at eternity. We say 'time flies,' but in reality it is we who fly, and as we pass on through eternity we mark our progress by time. It may be said that there is a certain relation between what we call time and the rate of motion of the different celestial bodies, but I don't think we can accurately measure a man's existence by means of motion. One year to the little child is as many years are to the man, and in the sight of God a thousand years are but as yesterday when it is past and as a watch in the night."

Mary started guiltily when Joy stopped speaking, and they all laughed. She had forgotten all about the making of character, and was very busy wondering what the folks at home, especially her father and Sam, would say about her engagement. She dreaded Sam's teasing most of all, and when Joy walked home with her that night she made him promise to tell no one of their engagement. She herself would tell her mother, but she did not wish her father or Sam to know.

CHAPTER XII.

ONE evening Twok was returning from a visit to Dr. Somerville, and in passing a barn that stood close to the roadside thought she heard someone moaning inside. Although it was beginning to grow dark and she was a little afraid, she climbed over the fence and entered the barn, for, she said to herself, someone might be hurt there. There was very little light inside, but she could see a man dangling from a beam with a rope about his neck. She looked at him for a moment in amazement and then with a scream of recognition cried,

"Oh, Jake, how could you?"

Then noticing a ladder reaching up to the beam from which the rope hung, she took in her hand a knife which lay on the floor, and climbing quickly up the ladder cut the rope. Jake's feet were only a few inches above the floor, and his body fell heavily against a stack of hay. In a moment Twok was beside him, opening his collar, rubbing his hands and calling him by name. Soon he opened his eyes. She had come just in time to save him.

"Is it you, Twok?"

"Yes. Oh, why did you do it?"

"Well, I've been unlucky since I was born. Came into the world the wrong way. You see my father and mother were not married. That made it wrong for me to be born. There's a right way and a wrong way of coming into this world, and the fellow that gets in the wrong way might as well give up at once, as there ain't no chance for him here. Don't see what difference it makes myself, but it's so. I came into this world the wrong way, without any fault of mine. I've been unlucky here, and now I'm going to start out fresh in the next world."

"I don't understand at all," said Twok, "but if there's a right way and a wrong way of coming into this world, perhaps there is a wrong way of getting into the next world. Suppose the right way is to die when your time comes. Why then you would get into heaven the wrong way if you killed yourself now, and everything would go wrong with you there the same as it has here. Just wait until it's time for you to die, and then you'll get into heaven the right way and everything will be happy. Besides, I'll soon be old enough to earn some money and I'll give it to you, because you were kind to me and saved me from the Law—from going to jail. I was a queer little girl then, and thought the Law was a monster that would eat me up. How funny! But I know better now, because Joy told me. Now promise never to try to kill yourself, again. There's a good Jake."

Jake promised and then she begged him to go home with her, to see how good and kind Joy and his mother were, assuring him that they would be very glad to see him and would give him such good things to eat that he wouldn't feel the least bit like dying. Jake was persuaded in spite of himself, and was led by the hand into Joy's workshop, looking for all the world like a great awkward boy who had done something wrong and was going to be punished for it. And Joy was not at all glad to see him, for he feared that Jake might claim Twok, but still he offered him a comfortable seat by the open fire and gave him one of his own coats in exchange for the ragged one he wore, and would have given him a pair of his shoes, only Jake's feet were too large. At tea time he made Twok's heart glad by heaping Jake's plate with the best things on the table; and when tea was over and Jake was sitting before the fire again, with Twok on a stool beside him, Joy pulled off his big boots for him, and said that although he was never apprenticed to shoe-making and couldn't mend a leather shoe as well as he could an iron one, still he was a sort of jack-of-all-trades and could mend shoes after a fashion. Then he cut up a pair of his own shoes, and patched Jake's with them in a way that would have been highly creditable to a shoemaker, and Jake stared with wonder until Twok explained that Joy could do everything. When it was bed time the young blacksmith insisted on giving up his bed to Jake, and lying down himself before the fire in his shop slept so soundly that he didn't wake up, about five o'clock next morning, when Jake got up, dressed and left the place without saying good-bye to anyone. But when he did wake up to find that Jake had gone, he examined everything very carefully to see that nothing was stolen, and was rather ashamed of his suspicions afterward when he found that everything was safe.

Twok cried a little when she heard of Jake's departure, and thought very anxiously about him for many months afterward, always remembering him night and morning in her prayers.

CHAPTER XIII.

"IF God made the world, who made God?" said Twok to Joy one wintry night about four years after her arrival, as she watched him mending a pair of skates for Alvin Linklater, who sat before the blazing fire waiting for them.

"What made you think of that just now, Twok?" said Joy.

"Alvin asked me one day a long time ago, and I couldn't tell him. Now he is here. You can tell him."

"Yes," said Alvin, "it is just as hard to suppose that God can exist without a creator as to imagine the world does."

"I think you are wrong," said Joy. "Geology not only shows very clearly that the world did not always exist, but describes the various stages of its formation; and all science teaches that the world is full of design. That proves that it was made. Now we know so little of God, that we can't prove that He did not always exist or that He was made. Knowing that the world was designed, we are sure that there must be a great designer. We have a God then, have we not?"

"Yes, I suppose so," said Alvin, doubtfully.

"Suppose we go still further back and assert what we cannot prove, that this God did not always exist—that He must have been designed and created. We merely fall back on a greater God, and so on for ever, until we attain almost to the idea of omnipotence. We cannot understand it. Is it any wonder? If we could fully understand God, would we not be almost co-equal with Him?"

"Well, you may be right, but even suppose there is a God, there are still any number of absurdities to be explained away. There's the question of the atonement, for example. I never could see how there could be anything in the mere fact of Christ's death that would save sinners. Can you explain that?"

"I'm not altogether orthodox on that point, Alvin; but if you have time to listen to an essay from my note-book, you will know what I think on the question of atonement."

"Fire away, Joy. You are great on essays, but I have lots of time."

Joy took out his note-book and read:

"THE ATONEMENT.

"It seems to me that a mistake is commonly made in regard to the atonement of Christ. The word atone, which is derived from at and one, means to set at one, and therefore, atonement or at-one-ment is a setting at one, or reconciliation. Now, according to the doctrine of the churches, the atonement was the setting of God at one with man, for they affirm that without the death of Christ it would be impossible for God to forgive man. Man still has the power to sin, and punishment is the natural result of sin, but God through the death of Christ has the power to forgive, which he lacked before. The logical outcome of this is that the object of Christ's death was to produce a change in the divine nature. But it seems to me that Christ's mission was not to effect a change in the nature of God, but to exert a mighty influence on the minds of men; an influence that would live through all ages and finally draw all men to him. God was always able and always willing to forgive; God was always loving and compassionate, but man through his ignorance and hardness of heart would not reciprocate that love. God and man can only be at one when the human will is in complete unison with the divine will, and God could not force man into unison with Him without destroying his free will—that is, his individuality. In destroying man's free will he would destroy the image and likeness of God. It being then impossible to force a man into unison with Him without destroying his divine nature, the only way open was to draw him ; and the strongest force of attraction is love. A peculiarity of this force, love, is that, in order that its power of attraction may be fully felt, the object of the attraction must know that he is loved : it is a full appreciation of love that induces love. Before the advent of Christ, men knew little about the nature of God. Having lived for ages without a personal knowledge of God, they had acquired a harsh, unjust idea of Him, and knowing His great powers, ascribed to Him many of the passions exhibited by men in highly exalted stations. Christ came to convey to the minds of men a true idea of their Creator, to show that God is love. Christ's mission was not to change the divine nature but to reveal it. Man was incapable of understanding the character of God until it was made manifest in Jesus. 'No man hath seen God at any time ; the only begotten Son, which is in the bosom of the Father, he hath declared Him.' Jesus in one of his talks with his disciples said, 'If ye had known me, ye should have known my Father also ; and from henceforth ye know Him and have seen Him.' And when Philip asked him to show them the Father he said, ' Have I been so long time with you and yet hast thou not known me, Philip ? He that hath seen me hath seen the Father ; and how sayest thou then, show us the Father? The words that I speak unto you I speak not of myself, but the Father that dwelleth in me He doeth the works. I am in my Father, and ye in me and I in you.' This is sometimes regarded as a statement by Christ that he was God, but it simply meant that the character of God was revealed through him, and just as he was at one with God by doing His will perfectly, so his disciples might be at one with God. No man could see the face of God and live, but the character of God was revealed to mankind in Christ Jesus, not fully revealed, for man could not understand it, but so far revealed as to serve as a guide to man in his relations with God and his fellow men. Although God could not show His face to men, He caused all His goodness to pass before them. A wrong idea of the atonement sometimes arises from a misconception of the nature of law—law, which is merely a mode of action of the divine will, being considered as something separate from God : something to which He had to sacrifice His son. The common belief is that, the punishment of sin being inevitable, all would perish had not Christ borne the punishment for us, so that on compliance with certain conditions we might be saved. It would seem impossible for Christ to be punished for sins as yet uncommitted, and so atone for the sins we commit to-day ; but, supposing this possible, Christ could not have expiated these sins except by suffering the full penalty, and therefore, in order to save man from eternal damnation by becoming his substitute, Christ must himself suffer eternal punishment. It was not from bodily death that he came to save them, and how could a death on the cross effect his purpose? And again if Christ bore the penalty of the transgressions of all mankind, all would be free from punishment notwithstanding their continuance in sin.

"Christ's whole teaching was the exposition of God's love ; he lived a life of loving sacrifice for men, his every word and action expressing his sympathetic love, and crowned this life of sacrifice by a death on the cross. Had it been otherwise —had he instead of submitting to death suffered himself to be made king—men, who are always disposed to criticise, might have said that his kindly actions arose from a desire for earthly power, but as it is there is nothing in his noble, loving life upon which critics can lay hold. It is to the teachings of Christ we should turn for information regarding his mission. Jesus himself did not teach that he was a substitute for us or that he was interceding with God for us. His teaching may be summed up in the few words recorded in the thirty-fifth verse of the thirteenth chapter of John, ' By this shall all men know that ye are my disciples, if ye have love one to another.' And when a sinful woman expressed her love for him by washing his feet with her tears and wiping them with her hair, he said, 'Her sins, which are many, are forgiven, for she loved much.' If there were any saving virtue in the mere act of dying, it would have been unnecessary for Christ to have said to his disciples, 'Go ye into all the world and preach the Gospel to every creature,' since all would be saved by Christ's death regardless of their ignorance. It is sometimes said that Christ died to atone for the original sin which is in us, but Jesus said, 'Suffer the little children to come unto me and forbid them not, for of such is the kingdom of heaven.' He evidently did not think there was any original sin. The little infant can no more be said to be sinful than the perfectly new piece of cloth can be said to be dusty. The new piece of cloth is not dusty, but it is liable to become dusty. The infant is not sinful, but it is liable to become so. Take away this liability to sin and you deprive man of his free will. Man has the power to remain pure or become smirched with sin, and the great aim of men and women should be to keep the little ones pure instead of waiting until they become all soiled and dusty, all smirched and spoiled with sin, and then endeavor to convert them. Some children have a greater tendency to become sinful than others. This at first sight seems hardly fair, but where a tendency to any particular sin is resisted, it strengthens the character, it strengthens the will and enables one to battle better with other evils. When a man with a naturally deceptive nature conquers this evil tendency, he is a better, stronger and nobler man than if he had remained truthful merely because he inherited from his parents a repugnance for falsehood."

"That was written some time ago," said Joy. "I will walk home with you and we will talk about it. Twok, you can either go to bed or wait until I return."

"I'll wait," said Twok. "Good-bye, Alvin."

While Joy was reading his essay, a number of villagers

were talking about him in a tavern not very far away. Since Twok's arrival, the villagers who had spent their evenings about the blacksmith's shop in the old days had gone to a neighboring tavern instead. They said Joy didn't seem to have so much time to talk to his friends now. What with his work and his books and his essays and his mother and this strange girl, his time was pretty well taken up without them, and so the tavern-keeper was the gainer. Public opinion, which in the old days was most favorable to Joy, was beginning to change. Why couldn't he send Twok to school like other children, and give a little of his spare time to entertaining his old friends, instead of trying to teach her everything himself? Afraid to have her associate with other children, they supposed. Fortunate thing for the other children, too. She came from one of the lowest haunts in Buffalo, and had vile manners. Swore terribly, it was said. No wonder that Joy had changed. There wasn't any particular harm in a boy swearing. They all did it more or less, but it was a different thing for a girl. Anyhow Joy wanted to know too much for a blacksmith. A blacksmith wasn't any better than anybody else, but Joy was beginning to hold himself above other people now, just because his father was a lawyer. It used to be so pleasant and cheerful to go and call on Joy, but now you felt somehow as if he were in a hurry to have you leave in order that he might go and look at that child and hear her swear. To be sure he did good work just the same as ever. He always did have a knack of seeing just what was wrong with anything out of order, and he always knew just how to fix it. The conversation about Joy was interrupted by someone remarking that Mrs. Slemmings had that morning given birth to twins, both boys. Then an old toper said that if Linklater village went on adding to its population at the same rate every day for ten years, it would be quite an important place at the end of that time, with a population of about eight thousand. This remark was greeted with great applause, and the villagers drank the health of the youngsters. Just as this ceremony was over Sam Slemmings entered the bar-room, and called for a drink in a loud voice.

"I suppose we'll not see much of you now," said one of the loungers. "You'll have to stay at home and nurse the babies."

"No, I don't. I'll break the darned things' heads first. Why there are thirteen of us now, and there won't be a dollar apiece for us, if they keep on coming at this rate."

At this speech, which would doubtless have greatly pleased the exponents of the Malthusian theory, there was a general laugh, and the man who had spoken before remarked that if the old man had any dollars to leave, Sam would no doubt see that he got a good share of them. Sam evidently considered this very complimentary and offered to treat the crowd to show that he got his share of them even now.

"They say you tried to kiss that girl of Joy Cougles, and he wouldn't let you. Is that so?"

"Oh, pshaw, that was about four years ago. She wasn't much more'n a baby then. If I wanted to kiss her now, he couldn't stop me."

"Your sister is going to marry him, they say."

"Not if I know it. My dad says she's not to go there after this week. There's enough for her to do to stay at home and mind the babies."

Sam buttoned up his coat, pulled his hat over his ears and went out into the night. As he opened the door, Joy and Alvin Linklater passed the tavern on their way to Alvin's home on the hill.

"He'll be gone an hour," said Sam to himself. "I'll have a look at the shop while he is gone. Perhaps she'll be there."

Sam was soon looking in at the window of Joy's shop. Mrs. Cougles was fast asleep in her room, and it would have been better for Twok if she had been sleeping by her side instead of sitting wide awake before the great fire in the workshop. He opened the door carefully, shut it softly, crept up to Twok and stooping over kissed her on the cheek.

Twok sprang up with fire in her eyes, looked at Sam angrily for a moment, and then deliberately took out her handkerchief and rubbed the kiss off with it. Sam caught her viciously in his arms, saying,

"I'll bite you this time instead of kissing you. I'll bite a hole in your cheek that you can't rub off, and it will make you so ugly that nobody will care to kiss you. There will always be a scar there."

"Oh, please don't," said Twok.

"Will you kiss me then?"

"No, I won't," said Twok emphatically, and as she spoke she snatched a red hot iron from the fire where Joy had left it and poked it into his face. It was well for Sam that the iron did not enter his eye. It cut a scar on the side of his face, which spoiled his beauty until his face was covered with a heavy beard which hid it. Sam screamed and Twok dropped the iron. Then seeing what she had done Twok was sorry, as she always was after being naughty.

"Oh, don't touch it," she cried as he put his hands up. "You will make it worse. I'll get some sweet oil."

There was oil and cotton batting in the cupboard close at hand, and she had them out in a moment. He submitted to having his face bound up by her, and she did it with gentle fingers and frequent exclamations of "poor boy!" But Sam did not stay any longer than was necessary, for he had no mind to meet Joy there.

When Joy came home and heard the story from Twok, he said sternly, with twitching mouth and twisting shoulder, that it served Sam right, and she need not waste any more tears over such a scoundrel.

CHAPTER XIV.

WHEN Sam reached home that night his sister Mary opened the door for him, and seeing his muffled face, exclaimed,

"Oh, Sam, what have you been doing?"

"You mind your own business and I'll mind mine. You'll wake dad up if you don't look out. I suppose you'd be glad enough to see me thrashed though."

"Oh, Sam!" she said reproachfully.

"You needn't 'oh' me, but just you remember this: If ever you do tattle and let dad know where I go at night, I'll run away and be a robber and a murderer."

"You know, Sam, that although it grieves me to have you go to the tavern, I wouldn't tell on you for anything."

She put up her mouth for a kiss, but he shoved her away roughly, saying,

"You'd better go and kiss the fellow that burned my face. You think more of him than you do of me."

"Oh, is your face burned? Who burned it?"

"You know well enough: it was that Joy Cougles."

"You must have been doing something very wicked then."

"No. I wasn't either. He stopped me from kissing Twok one day, so when I saw him kissing her in the shop I just thought I'd stop him, and then he up and burned my face with a red-hot iron."

Sam repeated this story to his father and mother and to everyone whom he met during the next few weeks. Mary doubted its truth, and when Twok asked her tearfully next morning how Sam was she questioned the child and learned all. Sam expected that she would hear Twok's story, but he relied on her love for him to prevent her telling the truth. When she reproached him with his untruthfulness, he told her he would murder Joy if she didn't shut up. That silenced her. He felt sure from what he knew of Joy that the young blacksmith would rather bear the blame than tell anyone that Twok did it, and Twok herself had so little communication with the villagers that she would never hear of it. But why should not he himself tell that Twok did it? Well, he was a young man of nearly eighteen years of age, and it would make him feel rather mean to have everyone pointing him out as the person who was scarred for life by a twelve-year-old girl whom he had tried to kiss against her will. Besides he had no ill-will toward Twok. He did feel like killing her when she poked the hot iron into his face, but then she was so sorry afterward and had bandaged his wounded face so tenderly, weeping quietly the while, and he believed she would have kissed him if he had asked her again before leaving the shop. Oh, no; Sam was not at all angry with Twok. So the villagers heard his story and, believing it, sympathized with him and grew very hard-hearted toward Joy. That was a turning point in the life of Sam Slemmings. He was never a boy again after the night on which Twok scarred his face. He began to think and plan as a man, and everyone noticed a great change in him. He examined into the details of his father's business transactions and discussed plans for his future. He avoided Joy Cougles, but planned meetings with Twok, with whom he seemed to be fascinated; and although he never had an opportunity to talk with her, he often met her on the road, and she always smiled sweetly and bowed most graciously on these occasions. Joy witnessed some of these meetings, and he began to imagine that Twok took as much pleasure in them as Sam did. This thought by no means pleased Joy. About this time Mary Slemmings left Linklater to attend the Wesleyan Ladies' College at Hamilton. So days and weeks and months passed by, and Twok was always growing in mind and body, and always working her way deep down into the hearts of those who knew her.

"What is the hammer saying to you this morning, Joy?" said Dr. Somerville, as he stopped at the shop of the young blacksmith on his way to visit a patient one day. "I hear seven regular beats, then a pause, then seven regular beats again, and so you keep it up. Each beat stands for a syllable, I know. What are the words in the sentence that your hammer is repeating over and over again?"

Joy looked up from his work, stopped the blows of the hammer and replied,

"God is Love and God is Law. That is what the hammer is saying to me this morning, and that is what it has been saying every day for a week past."

As Joy struck seven blows again, the doctor could almost hear the words ring out,

"God is Love and God is Law."

"The first part is familiar enough to me," said the doctor, "but how do you reason out the last part?"

"Why," said Joy, "many people believe that God, although usually acting in accordance with the laws of nature, sometimes works in opposition to them when He wishes to perform a miracle. God, say they, is omnipotent and can act either in accordance with or in opposition to the laws of nature as He pleases. This belief arises from a misconception of the nature of Law. Some people suppose the laws of nature to have been created by God, while others imagine them to be self-existent. We say 'God is Love;' why not also 'God is Law?' Laws are nothing but modes of action of the divine will. Now it is either possible that God may some day become fearfully wicked, or else it is a law that He cannot be otherwise than good; but if this is true and Law is something independent of God, it is more powerful than God and He is not omnipotent, or if Law is something created by God, the creature is greater than the creator. But if we suppose that God is Law, that Law is as much a part of His nature as love is the difficulty is obviated. That is why my hammer says, 'God is Love and God is Law.'"

"Well, I haven't your hammer to reason with and I'll have to turn the thing over in my brain as I drive along to-day. But, Joy, how is business now? How is that new blacksmith's shop affecting your trade? There are three blacksmiths in the village now. You used to have a monopoly of almost everything except horse-shoeing, which you never did. Three blacksmiths are a little too many for one small village."

"I can't say that I have much to do, and I find it difficult sometimes to make both ends meet, although Twok does all the housework now and takes care of my mother. The people don't seem to like me as well as they used. Still there are many things that the other fellows don't know how to fix. They have to come to me for them. But if I had no one to think of except myself, I would go to one of the big cities."

"What do you suppose is the reason for the change in popular sentiment? The people here almost worshipped you at one time."

"I can't imagine."

"Perhaps the way you branded Sam Slemmings has something to do with it."

"I didn't do that."

"Ah! Well, I didn't believe the whole of Sam's story. I thought you must have had strong provocation, but still I am glad to know that you didn't do it at all. But how was it done?"

"It was Twok who did it, and it served him right; but don't you tell anyone that. I would rather have him lie about me than about her."

"How did it happen?"

Joy repeated what Twok had told him, and defended her action. "But what I hate worst of all," he said in conclusion, "is that Twok, who seemed to hate the very sight of him before that night, seems now to have taken a great fancy for the branded brute. She cried herself to sleep over him that night and made anxious inquiries for weeks afterward. When she meets him now she gives him one of her sweetest smiles, and I believe she prays every night and morning that the scar may leave his face."

The doctor smiled. The day before he had witnessed a meeting between Sam and Joy and Twok, who were walking together. Joy had scowled fiercely while his mouth twitched furiously; Twok had smiled sweetly and bowed most gracefully, and Sam had lifted his hat without looking at Joy, but after passing had turned around and shaken his fist at him. The doctor smiled for a moment at the recollection and then looked very grave as he said,

"Well, Joy, one story that s going the rounds of the village is false then, but I'm afraid the other is true."

"What is it?" said Joy excitedly. "Nothing about Twok and Sam?"

"No," said the doctor, "it is about yourself. They say your character has changed. You are not the same cheerful Joy to whom everybody used to tell their troubles. You are just as kind and tender and careful of your sweet little mother as you ever were, and no one could have been more kind to Twok; but still there is something lacking now that you once had, a something that made everyone feel at peace with the world when with you. I can't tell what it was, but it was something very pleasant, and I'm afraid it will never come back. Peace and hate cannot live together, and I believe that hate of Sam Slemmings has driven the peace out of your heart. You were never very orthodox, I know; but you used to be a great believer in prayer as a moral power. Do you ever pray that you may have kindly feelings toward Sam Slemmings?"

"No, I don't want to like him. I believe we have both hated each other ever since one day years ago when I found him kicking his pretty sister Mary, because she wouldn't tell a lie to save him from a whipping. She didn't intend to tattle, you understand. She never did that. But he invented a story which he knew no one would believe out of his own mouth, and so tried to force her to tell it for him. I gave him a thrashing that day, I can tell you, which I think he will remember to his dying day."

"But you didn't feel toward him then as you do now?"

"Well, perhaps not just the same, but that was the beginning of it. He is even a greater brute now than he was then."

The doctor went his way, whistling contemplatively, and Joy resumed his work, but the strokes did not fall any more that morning with the regular pauses that always marked them when he was pounding a proposition of any kind into his head. When night came on he was cheerful again, and having a job to finish worked away with a will. It was a piece of work that required a great deal of constant hammering and Twok, listening, heard the regular pauses at long intervals and went out to the workshop.

"It's a long sentence this time," she cried. "I can't guess what it is. What is the hammer saying, Joy?"

"The sum of the cosines of two angles is equal to twice the product of the cosine of half the sum of the angles into the cosine of half their difference."

"I wish you would make the hammer say something that I can understand. I sometimes think you have a peculiar way of striking for some words, so when sentences are short I can often guess them. Now I always know when you hammer my name."

"Do you, Twok?"

"Why, yes. You were hammering me all to pieces early this morning. What was the hammer saying about me?"

"The hammer wasn't saying anything bad about you, Twok, but I can't always tell you just what it says. I don't always know very well myself. Sometimes I forget all about the hammer as I work, lost in thought, and then suddenly wake up to find that my thought is shaping itself into words and the hammer is pounding it out."

CHAPTER XV.

ONE day Dr. Somerville said to Joy, "You are pretty well up in classics and mathematics, and you have a pithy way of telling what you know. Why not turn your knowledge to account by giving private lessons?"

"Easier said than done. Where am I to get the pupils?"

"I have already secured one for you to begin with."

"Who?"

"Sam Slemmings."

"Sam Slemmings?"

"Yes, Sam Slemmings. Now don't be a fool, Joy Cougles. I'm ashamed of you. Why shouldn't you teach Sam Slemmings, if you are well paid for it?"

"What can Sam Slemmings want with classics and mathematics?"

"His father wants to make a lawyer of him, and he thinks you can coach him for the matriculation better than anyone else in the village."

"Well, suppose I can. I'm not going to assist in making a snob out of a brutal butcher boy."

"Come, come, Joy. You might save enough to take you to the University at Toronto, if you get a few pupils. If you refuse to take Sam, you will make an enemy of his father and he will use all his influence to prevent other people sending you pupils. He will pay you six dollars a week for three hours a day, and Sam will come to you. Now that times are slack, you can easily spare three hours a day."

"If I can't get to the University without giving lessons to him, I'll stay at home and be a blacksmith."

"Twok might take music lessons, Joy. You know she fairly loves music. And your mother might have one of those easy chairs that you were admiring so much in Hamilton the other day and wishing that you could afford to buy."

"Well, hang it all, Doctor, I'll do it. Send him on."

Dr. Somerville hurried away as if afraid Joy might change his mind. Now the worthy doctor had troubled himself greatly about the change in Joy, and had thought if he could only contrive to bring him and Sam together in a friendly way, everything would soon be restored to its old satisfactory basis. So when the wealthy butcher told him he was going to make a lawyer of Sam and asked whom he should engage to coach the young man, he at once thought of Joy, feeling sure that if the young blacksmith could be induced to teach Sam he would soon stop hating him, for Joy, he knew, would conscientiously carry out his contract if he undertook to teach the youth, and he had an idea that when Sam, who was not at all dull, began to make progress his tutor would grow proud of him, and he argued that a person could not very well hate anyone in whom he took pride. Dr. Somerville did not in the least think of doing good to Sam in making this arrangement. He did not care a straw about Sam. But Joy had been his model boy. He had calculated on living to see him an ideal man, and he was not going to have all his plans spoiled because a fellow like Sam came in the way and made Joy hate him. Of course he could easily persuade the butcher to send Sam away where Joy could not see him, but what good would that do? The only thing that would make Joy right again was a victory over himself. So the doctor told the butcher that Joy was the man for the place, and that no other man in Canada could give Sam such thorough teaching.

"What!" said the butcher. "Him that branded my boy like as if he were a sheep? You don't catch me sending Sam to him."

"But Joy didn't do that?"

"What do you mean?"

"I mean what I say. Joy Cougles never touched an iron, hot or cold, to Sam's face. Your boy is an infernal liar, and told the story to get himself out of a scrape. Now you needn't look angry. He'll make all the better lawyer for being a good liar, and you know it. There is no use trying to fool me, Mr. Slemmings. Between you and me, you wouldn't have half so many dollars in the bank, nor own nearly so many corner lots in Toronto, if you were not pretty good at lying yourself. Ha, ha!" and the doctor slapped the butcher on the back and laughed immoderately, as if it were the best joke of the season.

"How much will it cost?" said the butcher.

"Probably about six or seven dollars a week for three hours a day."

"Thunder and lightning! I can't spend no six or seven dollars a week on educating that boy."

"Must give up the idea of making a lawyer of him then."

"Well, I could send him to the Hamilton Collegiate Institute for less than that."

"Yes. That's a good school, but he would only be in a class with other boys, most of them much younger than himself, and wouldn't get along half so fast as with Joy Cougles, who is a born teacher. What you want is somebody who can coach him for that matriculation examination in short time. The older he grows the more valuable his time will be to him and to you. So you will gain rather than lose by shoving him through in a hurry, even if it is expensive. Besides, after he has matriculated, you will have to put him into a lawyer's office, and it will take five years to make a full fledged lawyer. Hurry him up."

"I guess you're right, Doctor, and there's another reason why I would like to have Joy Cougles teach Sam. I'm going out of the meat business this month, and when my boy's a great lawyer living in Toronto, I don't want folks to throw it up in his face that his sister Mary used to work as kitchen maid for them Cougles. He can say to anybody that insults him that way, "Sir, you're mistaken. Mrs. Cougles was a poor cripple that my sister used to go to attend out of kindness, and my father out of kindness hired Joy to teach me Latin and such like. How's that, Doctor, eh?"

"Exactly, exactly," said the doctor. "You always were a clever liar. You ought to have been a lawyer yourself, although I don't know that you could have made much more out of law than you have out of meat. But when Joy has matriculated that boy for you and he gets a little legal training, the two of you together will make a clever team. Oh, a fine team, I can tell you."

And the doctor and the butcher shook hands very heartily as they parted. Dr. Somerville went away rubbing his hands with satisfaction to have the interview with Joy already recorded in this chapter. That interview would have come to a very different conclusion if Joy had heard the conversation between the butcher and the doctor which preceded it.

CHAPTER XVI.

SAM was very much pleased with his father's plan of patronizing the Cougles, but he was not a fool and knew that it would not do to put on any patronizing airs before Joy yet. He did not wish to study Latin or Greek or Euclid or anything else, but he did wish to be a lawyer, and was willing to endure some drudgery for the sake of that. Besides, he would have a chance to see Twok often. What a pretty girl she was ! Just the sort of a girl for a lawyer's wife. So bright and quick. She would make a great many friends, and a lawyer needed friends. Just the right age, too. He would not wish to marry for four or five years, and by that time she would be eighteen or nineteen he thought. It was Saturday, and Sam was to begin lessons on Monday. He was walking along the road when he met Twok, going to call on the doctor. She bowed and smiled; he lifted his hat. Sam was beginning to look stylish, she thought, and he would be really handsome if it were not for that scar. And how big he was getting to be; she was only a mite beside him. Sam passed her a little way, and then turning round and walking fast overtook her.

" May I walk with you, Miss ———— "

" Jakwok," prompted Twok.

" May I have the pleasure of walking with you, Miss Jakwok ? "

" Yes, if you like."

" I do wish very much to do so, for I want to tell you how sorry I am that I used to treat you so rudely when I was a boy."

Sam spoke as if the time when he was a boy were a very long way back in the past, and Twok began to feel old, too.

"Well, I'm sure I treated you meanly enough to pay for it," and Twok looked at the scar on his face as if she had half a mind to have a good cry over it.

"Oh, never mind. My beard will cover that all up in a few years. But I really was only fooling when I said I'd bite you that night. Of course it was very rude, but I was only a boy then, Twok—I beg your pardon—Miss Jakwok."

"You can call me Twok, if you like. I like my friends to call me that."

"Then I'm at last installed as one of your friends, Twok, dear?"

"Oh, I didn't tell you to call me dear."

"But you must be dear to all your friends."

"Yes, I suppose so; but you mustn't say it. It isn't proper."

"I begin to take lessons from Joy on Monday."

"I heard something about it. You couldn't have a better master."

"Yes, he will do very well for a while, until I matriculate. After that I will, of course, soon know much more than he does, for he is only a blacksmith. I will be a great lawyer."

Now take care what you are about, Sam Slemmings. You have succeeded admirably with your courtship so far, but have a care, Sam. Listen to that little girl's answer and learn to be cautious.

"Oh, it's best not to be too confident. It will take you years and years to learn anything like so much as Joy knows. Good-bye; I'm going in to see the doctor."

The doctor and his wife were both at home, and they gave her a hearty welcome.

"And what makes you so quiet to-day, Doctor?" said Twok after she had talked with Mrs. Somerville for a little while. "You sit there looking out of the window as if you didn't care one bit for the girl who has come to see you."

"I'm thinking of my hobby, Twok."

"Couldn't you persuade them to adopt it in the Hamilton schools? It would soon spread if it were once established there."

"But I'm thinking of my other hobby, Twok."

"Why, I never knew before that you had two. I'm so sorry for you, Doctor. You must be awfully worried. I'm almost moved in pity to offer to take one from you, but I fear it would be too great a burden for one so young."

"Why, now I think of it, you might help me somewhat with my hobby."

"Which one, Doctor? Not that one you told me about before. You surely cannot wish me to begin pronouncing words the way they are spelled. I'll say col-o-nel instead of kur-nel when I'm with you, if you like; but please do not ask me to say it to anybody else."

"It isn't that hobby I mean. It's the other one. It's the one I love best. It's Joy."

"Joy?"

"Yes."

"Why, then if it's Joy, it must be my hobby, too. But explain yourself, sir. Don't keep me in such a state of curiosity any longer."

"You came to Joy a little girl and you are almost a lady now, just as tall as many ladies are, and your hair is growing very long. You are going to be a lovely woman, Twok."

"Yes, but about Joy," said Twok, impatiently.

"Give me time, child. I'm coming to Joy in a moment."

"Yes, but you keep wasting your time talking about me, when I want to hear about him."

"What I was going to say is, that you have known Joy a long time, and he has been a very good brother to you; but I have known him longer still, and love him as if he were my own son. When I first knew him he was a little boy, but he had the fortitude of a man. His father was killed by an accident and Joy thought he must take his place. He must be both husband and son to his mother. You know how weak she is. She was never strong, and after Joy was born she was weaker still. She never seemed to have any strength after that, and for the life of me I can't tell how she has lived all these years. I think her love for Joy has sustained her. Joy says that although love and life are the two commonest things, nobody understands them. I guess he is right. Perhaps they are somewhat akin. Anyhow I never could understand why it is that while great strong organisms often yield to the most ordinary diseases or the most trifling accident, a little delicate woman like that can live on for years. But if she has lived for Joy, I think she owes her life to him in other ways as well. He has been so careful of her. That little boy would wait on her and rub her aching head until the pain all went out of her head into his hand, and arms. Have you ever had a headache, Twok? No. Then you don't know how much magic there is in those hands of his. Well, she was very subject to headaches then. Much more so then than now, and many an afternoon Joy has rubbed her head while other boys were out doors playing ball. He never learned to play ball or any other boyish games, although he became an expert swimmer, a good runner and jumper, an accomplished horseman and took lessons in boxing from a broken-down boxing master who brought up in Linklater as a last resort. Joy was more of a man at six years of age than Sam Slemmings was at sixteen. But he had one great fault: he had naturally a very hot temper. He was never angry with his mother; he was all gentleness with her and before her. But away from her he had an awful temper, and his testy old grandfather seemed to delight in arousing his anger. He was an honest old man and I believe he liked the boy well enough, but he had a very ugly habit of saying mean things to him. I really was afraid that Joy would kill someone some day while in a passion, and I didn't know what to make of a union of such gentleness with such violence. I do not think he could have kept it up very long, for either the one or the other must have conquered. I used to watch him with a sort of dread and you may be sure I talked to him more than once, for I felt certain that he would be either a very good man or a very bad one. On his twelfth birthday he came to me with such a bright expression on his face. Oh, Twok, you have seen it. You know what it was like. He said to me, 'Doctor, I have had a big fight with the devil to-day, and I have beaten him. He always beat me before, but now I've got him down once, I think I can do it again. He'll probably come at me again, but after I have beaten him a good many times, he will become afraid of me and let me alone.' I never saw him in a passion again. It was a hard fight sometimes, and his face would twitch nervously as if he were in pain, but he always came off victorious. One day I said to him, 'What do you knock him over with, Joy?' And he answered, 'Prayer.' When I saw that little fatherless boy wrestling with the devil out in the workshop, and then nursing his mother so tenderly in her sick room, I began to make a hobby of him. I said to myself, 'He is a model boy. He will make an ideal man.' And he grew to be a man whom everybody loved—a handsome man, tall and strong of body and of noble face. He was just the same to all. Everybody seemed to feel that he was the one in whom to confide—they've always got to have a confessor of some sort; before they went to Joy they came to me. And now, Twok, they come to me again. They don't go to him any more. They think he has changed, and so he has. I'm afraid the devil is going to get him after all those years of fighting."

Twok interrupted here with a great sob, which she choked down to say,

"I don't believe it. You go and set up an impossible ideal and worship it, and then because Joy fails to come quite up to it, you say the devil has got him. Why should Joy be so much better than other men? This hobby of yours is a great deal worse than the other one. I don't like it one bit."

"There, Twok, don't cry. You will lose all your pretty looks."

"Then why will you be so hateful?"

'But he hates Sam Slemmings."

"Oh, pshaw! He doesn't like him. But who would? The conceited thing!"

"He told me that he hated Sam, and said he wouldn't pray against it, because he didn't want to like him."

"Then why do you bring them together as master and pupil, just to torment him?"

"Because I want to see Joy knock the devil down in another stand-up fight."

"How absurd!"

"I wish you would take him in training, Twok, and make him pray. You pray yourself, I know."

"Yes, but what can I do? He hammers poor little me to pieces every morning, and he never will tell me what the hammer is saying about me."

CHAPTER XVII.

ON the afternoon of the following day, as Twok was washing the dinner dishes, often glancing furtively at Joy, who was reading Dickens' "Little Dorrit," there was a rap on the door and Mary Slemmings entered.

"Oh, Mary!" said Twok, "I'm so glad to see you. I have been expecting you all day, and Joy must have been dying with impatience, although he said nothing."

"On the contrary I was not expecting her. I thought she was at the college in Hamilton."

"Why, Joy, I told you about a week ago that she would be home this Sunday. It must have gone in one ear and out of the other. I told you one morning after you were pounding me until my bones ached with the noise."

"Pounding you?" said Mary.

"Yes. Isn't it mean? He has a way of saying things with his hammer. Did you never notice it?"

"No."

"Why, I did a week after I came. That is the way he learned his Greek verbs and enunciations in Euclid and lots of other things. He would hammer them over and over until he couldn't forget them. Then sometimes the hammer would say things that I could understand, and I would be so pleased. I liked it ever so much. But I don't like it a bit now, because he won't tell me why he hammers my name so often."

"How queer you talk, Twok! I can never notice any difference in the way he hammers. You have such an imagination," and Mary looked at Joy as if she felt a little hurt at his indifference regarding her whereabouts.

"Come to my room and take off your things. What a pretty dress you have on! You look lovely. Do the girls like Dr. Burns as well as Dr. Rice?"

"Oh, they are so different, that you can't compare them. They say Dr. Burns has something the same idea as Joy about the atonement ; not just the same, but something the same. I heard a gentleman say the other day that he would be expelled from some churches for holding such views."

"Well, I'm sure they will be very foolish if they expel him. Joy says the church that is most tolerant in this age of thinking will be the most successful. He says no two men can think exactly alike on all points, and it is the endeavor to make them all think alike that divides the church into so many sects. All men who love one another are Christians because Jesus said, ' By this shall all men know that ye are my disciples, if ye have love one to another.' If they would found the church on what Christ said instead of on what his disciples said, there might be a united Christian church. Do you take music lessons, Mary?"

"Yes, I'm taking lessons from Professor Ambrose."

"Oh, I wish I could. But, Mary, Dr. Somerville says they talk such slang at the college, that he wouldn't have a daughter of his there. He says one English language is enough for him if it were only pronounced correctly, and he can't see what's the use of girls learning to talk slang—I believe he talks slang himself sometimes. But they don't teach it there, do they?"

"Oh, Twok, how simple you are! They teach us to speak beautifully, and we study English, the best authors. But of course the girls talk slang in their rooms. However, they don't all do it. Sam comes to see me often. He has been taking lessons in dancing and deportment. It is improving him wonderfully. I never saw such a change in a boy."

"He *is* improving," said Twok.

"I do wish Joy would study law, Twok. His father was a lawyer and he is so clever himself. They would make him a great judge some day."

"You think a good deal of him, don't you, Mary?"

"Oh, Twok!"

"Why of course you do, and why shouldn't you? He is fond of you, Mary, too, but he isn't one who shows his feelings as some people do. You will make a handsome couple. I will have *such* a time nursing your children. And, oh, Mary, Joy and I will teach them what the hammer is saying."

Was that a pang of pain at your heart, Mary? Surely you do not care for what the hammer says. But why did the color leave your blushing face so suddenly when Twok spoke of the hammer?

The two girls went out to Mrs. Cougles' room, where Joy had seated himself by the bed. Mary kissed the cripple affectionately, and then turning to Joy said,

"Have you finished your interesting book?"

"Not exactly, Mary, but I have read it before. It is 'Little Dorrit.' I like it best of Dickens' novels."

"Some people say it is a great waste of time to read novels. What do you think?"

"Oh, there are silly novels and bad novels, just as there are silly people and bad people; but I've learned a great deal from good novels. They are often better than sermons. Then they give you a wider experience of life. The characters of a first class novel are real. When I say they are real, I do not mean that they are copied from life. An author of genius is not a copyist, but a creator. His characters are like men, and yet unlike any man. Just as every real person is different from every other person, so every real creation of a novelist is different from anyone who ever lived either in a book or out of it. And yet the characters of a novel must be so nearly like the characters in other books and in real life, that they will seem natural. So we make a great many new acquaintances by reading novels. But the best thing of all about them, I think, is that they take us out of ourselves. We are all very selfish and never fully sympathize with one another. Even our love and sympathy is selfish to a large extent. We love our friends in their relations with us, not in their relations with other people. But in reading a novel we go out of ourselves altogether. We put ourselves in the places of the characters of a novel as we never put ourselves in the places of real persons, and it does us good to go entirely out of ourselves for a little while and truly feel the joys and sorrows, hopes and fears of other people."

"Oh, Joy, how do you think such things?" said Mary, but Twok said,

"I think you are wrong, Joy. Not about the making of characters, but about the selfishness. You say we put ourselves in the places of the characters. Yes, but how do we do it? Very selfishly, I think. It is not with all the characters that we sympathize, but only with one or two; and we follow those characters through the story, selfishly wishing them to come out all right, regardless of the other people in the story. We don't always pick out the best characters, either. We just settle down into the place of the character that the author has wrapt his own selfishness about. Now look at Martin Chuzzlewit. That dear Tom Pinch was worth fifty thousand Martin Chuzzlewits, and he loved Mary better than Martin did, too. We ought to be very angry because Mary didn't fall in love with him and marry him, but we just settle down wherever Dickens puts us and are selfishly satisfied. Of course we pity Tom and love him, but it is something the same sort of pity one would have for the person whom he ousted from a nice situation in an office, in order that he might secure it himself. Of course he feels sorry for the poor fellow who has lost the place. He even wishes that there were another place just like it, in order that both might be satisfied; but it is awfully mean all the same."

"I never saw two such people," said Mary. "It is really time for me to go."

They persuaded her to stay to tea, and the three sat down to the table, Mrs. Cougles not being well enough to leave her bed. Joy was about to help Mary to some fruit, when she said,

"You haven't said grace."

"We never have any when his mother is in bed. She always says it," said Twok.

"He ought to learn then," said Mary.

"Couldn't you say something, Joy?" said Twok.

"Yes, if it will give you any satisfaction. I don't see any reason to thank God for providing this meal, because if we suppose He provides for us, we must wonder why He doesn't provide for some other people who haven't enough to eat. I think there are wise laws which are God's ways, and one of them is that He allows us to provide our own meals; but I can say grace if it will please you."

They bent their heads and he said, "Lord, help us so to eat, that the good things we have provided for ourselves will do us good instead of harm."

"Joy!" exclaimed Twok reproachfully as he finished, and Mary said, "I would rather you wouldn't say anything than be so irreverent."

"There is nothing irreverent in that," said Joy. "It is more important how we eat than what we eat."

"You think," said Twok, "that Jesus was wise and good, and did not he give thanks before taking food or offering it to others? Then you have said that The Lord's Prayer is the most complete of all prayers, and it says, 'Give us this day our daily bread.' Surely if it is right to ask for bread it is right to return thanks. It seems to me that the object of it is to keep it continually in our minds that we ought to be grateful to God for all the blessings of life. Though in Him we live and move and have our being, we are too apt to feel as if we were quite independent of Him."

Soon after tea Mary said she must go. As she was putting on her overshoes she said to Twok,

"I do wish my feet were as small as yours. What size do you take?"

"I wear twos," said Twok, "but you see I'm not as tall as you are, nor so stout, and my feet ought to be smaller. I don't believe that I am going to grow any more. I get Joy to measure me once a month, and for the last three months I have not grown a particle. I was growing very fast before. I am just five feet, three inches. Joy is five feet ten inches."

"You look taller, Twok, because you are so slender. I am five feet six, but I'm sure I don't look three inches taller than you do."

Mary being ready kissed Twok good-bye, and she and Joy went out softly, that they might not disturb Mrs. Cougles, who had fallen asleep.

"It is over three years since we were first engaged, is it not?" said Joy, after they had walked some distance along the road in silence.

"Yes," said Mary.

"You did not wish me to say anything to your father or Sam at the time."

"No, but I told my mother."

"I expected to have saved a good deal of money by this time. Three years seems a long time when you look ahead, but very short when you look back, and I'm poorer now than I was then. If you marry me, you will have to take a poor man."

"I will have some money myself. My father is rich."

"Yes, but he doesn't like me, and neither does Sam. He won't give you much if you marry me. Besides, I would never be content living on my wife's money. Sam is going to be a lawyer, and you should have an equally good position. You are beautiful and rich, and will have a good education when you finish your course at Hamilton. With all these things in your favor you will have lots of chances to marry a professional man in a good position. It seems like throwing yourself away to marry a common blacksmith, who is losing what trade he has."

"You are not common if you are a blacksmith."

"You will not be able to go into society if you marry me. Even your brother Sam would be ashamed to invite you to his house after he is a full fledged lawyer, if you were only a blacksmith's wife. He is already ashamed of the fact that your father was a butcher, and will be angry if you connect yourself with other than a professional or business man of standing. He will say that you are keeping him back."

"When a woman promises to marry a man, she means to give up everyone else if necessary."

"But when a woman marries a poor man, she has far the worst of the bargain. The man has his regular hours of work during the day and rests in the evening, but the woman slaves always from early morning until late at night, keeping the house in order, cooking, washing dishes, caring for the children, darning socks, mending clothes and hundreds of other little things that seem but trifles when mentioned separately, but which when taken together make up a life of toil and weariness that makes the majority of women old before their time and drives some of them crazy."

They had reached the gate of Mr. Slemmings' place, and Joy said good-bye and then hurried home. An hour afterward Twok sat on a stool at Joy's feet. He was on a low rocking chair.

"Joy," she said, breaking a silence which had lasted for some time.

"Yes, Twok."

"I have been thinking of what you said a long time ago about character making. You are making your own character now. Do you hate Sam?"

"I'm afraid so, Twok."

"Oh Joy, you make me feel so sorry."

"Do you care so very much for him?"

"Care for him? I detest the sight of him."

"Why, then, I might possibly get to like him better."

"How spiteful you are, Joy?"

"But how can I help hating him when I remember how he used to kick and beat Mary because she wouldn't tell lies for him, and how he would bully all the little boys at school, and how he poisoned Lion, and told outrageous lies about you and me, and—and when I see him making love to you."

"But Joy, you can hate his wickedness without hating him, and I really think he is better than he used to be."

"But I can't separate his wickedness and meanness from him. There isn't such a thing as wickedness in the abstract."

"Well, then, you can wish and pray that he may grow to be good."

"O Twok! I am more wicked than I thought. You understand me better than I do myself. I can't even wish that he may become good. The devil has got at me in a new way."

"Couldn't you knock him down with prayer? You did it once. I will pray for you, too."

"Oh, my little Twok! It will be very sweet to me to have you praying for me, but it cannot do me any good. The only prayers that can help a man to conquer himself are his own prayers, and I somehow can't pray now. I begin, but stop before I'm through, feeling that I'm only saying words. If I felt what I was saying, there would be no need of saying it. The thing would be done."

"My poor, poor boy," said Twok, beginning to cry softly, while her long hair as if in sympathy broke from its fastenings and fell in disorder about her, almost covering her. Then a thought seemed to strike her and she started up, drying her tears, snatching up her hair, giving it a twist, throwing it over her shoulder, and saying in a voice that sounded certain of success,

"Joy, you forgot that he is Mary's brother. *You* can't hate *her* brother."

But this argument, strong as it seemed to Twok, had no effect on Joy, and so she gave it up as something beyond her and busied herself in making Mrs. Cougles comfortable. But when she kneeled down by the bed that night the only thing she said was, "God, please help my poor boy to pray," and after she was in bed her heart kept saying the same thing over and over as it throbbed in her bosom until she fell asleep.

CHAPTER XVIII.

AT the breakfast table next morning, as Twok poured out the coffee, she glanced at Joy's face and then excitedly dropping the cup of hot coffee on the carpet, cried,

"Oh, Joy, I'm so glad! My prayers did do good."

"Why, Twok, how do you know?"

"Can't I read you like a book? Didn't you say yesterday that I understood you better than anyone else? Oh, I know. Mary will be delighted."

"I don't see what Mary has to do with it."

"Well, I do. It will make her happy. I hope my breaking the cup didn't wake your mother up. It is too bad for me to break the things you work so hard to buy. I must be a great expense to you, but I haven't broken very many dishes, have I, Joy?"

"Very few, Twok. You are the best housekeeper in Linklater."

"Not better than Mary?"

"Yes, better than Mary. You are no neater, for she is a model of neatness. In that respect she equals you, and I don't think she ever broke a dish; but you are brighter, Twok. I don't know how you do it, but you have a knack of touching a thing here and moving a thing there that alters the whole appearance of a room. I can't imagine where you learned it, but I think my mother would have been like that if she were strong like you."

"Oh, Joy, isn't she lovely? Have you read in the papers about these faith cures? Couldn't we do something for her?"

"I am afraid not. Dear little mother! I wish she could get well. I sometimes fear that she will not live long. She is so very weak. I don't think anything can be done for her. I can conceive of certain sorts of diseases or weaknesses being cured by faith—the effect of mind on matter—but I'm afraid that a case like her's couldn't."

"Oh, dear, what a pity!"

"You are to take music lessons, Twok."

"You can't afford it."

"Yes, I can. I will get six dollars a week for teaching Sam."

"And you dislike him so much. It is too bad that you should be tormented just for me. Oh, no, I forgot. You don't hate him now."

"No, Twok, not now. I hope it will never come again, but perhaps the fight is not over yet. Do you remember what I carved on the stone over Lion's grave?"

"Yes. It was horrid."

"Well, I smoothed it off early this morning, and really while I was doing it I wished that he might become a good man, and I am going to do my best to push him forward with his studies. You are my good angel, Twok. But for you I might still have hated him. I may sometimes find the old feeling coming up, but I'll fight hard against it."

Sam came and went that day and many others. He was ignorant for his age, never having paid much attention to his studies while at school; but now he worked hard and learned rapidly, and Joy did grow rather proud of his pupil's advancement. He began to watch the boy and study his character with a queer sort of interest. Twok took music lessons twice a week, and practiced every day on Mrs. Somerville's piano for six months. At the end of that time she came to Joy one day, and said,

"I'm not going to take music lessons any more."

"Why?"

"Because it isn't fair. You are to be married to Mary in about a year and a half, and need all the money you can save."

"But you are making such wonderful progress. It would be a shame to stop now."

A very determined look came into Twok's eyes, and she said,

"I have thought and thought about it, and my mind is made up. It would not be right, but I'll be able to practice just the same."

When she went to take her usual practice that day, she knocked at the door of the doctor's study and was admitted.

"I have stopped taking lessons," she said.

"What's that for?"

"I have been thinking how much Joy has spent on me, and I can never pay him back. He isn't saving anything, and it will soon be time for him to marry Mary."

"Marry Mary?"

"Yes. Didn't you know? I thought of course he told you. I suppose I should not have told it then. Just now the mother needs me, but when Mary comes she can do everything. Will you try to get me a place somewhere then?"

"What sort of a place?"

"I would make a good house maid. I wouldn't like it much, as it is considered a menial position; but if I can't get anything else to do, I'll be that. Perhaps I might be a governess. I never went to school, but Joy has taught me quite a bit, and I could teach little children. I wish I could make enough to pay Joy back."

"My dear child, years ago Mrs. Somerville tried to persuade me to coax you away from Joy and his mother to be our own daughter, but I wasn't mean enough to do it. We both love you as well as ever now, and just so soon as Joy and his mother can spare you I want you to come and live with us. In the meantime go on with your music lessons. I will give you money or lend it to you, if you prefer to be independent, and you can pay it back some time when you are a great music teacher or a celebrated cantatrice."

So she went on with her music lessons, practicing diligently during all the hours she could spare from her house work and waiting on Mrs. Cougles, who grew weaker every day. Joy worked and studied and taught, and made his hammer talk just the same as ever for a year, and Twok never learned what the hammer was saying about her. Then one day when Sam came to take his lessons as usual he was met by Twok, who closed the door very gently and stood outside with him while she said,

"Sam, he cannot teach you to-day. His mother is very weak, and the doctor is alarmed. Joy sits by her night and day, never sleeping. But he says you do not need any more teaching for that examination. You cannot fail to pass honorably. He thinks you are very clever and is quite proud of you."

Twok put out her little hand. He took it and said,

"Are you proud of me? That is what I care most about?"

"We are all proud of you," said Twok, and then she went into the house.

Sam walked away with springing step and a light heart, while Joy and Twok watched by the bedside of Mrs. Cougles with very heavy hearts. The doctor said she might live twenty-four hours, considering her extraordinary vitality, but if it were anyone else he would say six. She was too weak to talk and seldom even opened her eyes, but once she did look up and smiled at Joy, who sat on the edge of the bed with one of her hands in his, and Twok, who sat on a chair beside the bed. She did not seem quite satisfied, and tried to speak. Joy, watching her lips, said,

"Do you mean Twok to give me her hand?"

She smiled approvingly, and Twok accordingly placed her hand in Joy's. So Joy and Twok watched together, Joy holding his mother's hand with his right and clasping Twok's with his left. The clock seemed to tick louder than it ever ticked before, and Twok looking at the swinging pendulum almost wondered whether it would stop when the dying woman's pulse ceased to throb, and all the time there was a dull pain at her heart, but her eyes were dry and bright, and the little hand in Joy's left was very warm, while that in his right was growing cold. The pulse throbs stopped long before the six hours were counted off, but the clock went right on ticking, and Joy sat still with the dead hand chilling his right hand and the live one burning in his left, and Twok thought the mother was sleeping, until the doctor came and led them both away.

[END OF PART I.]

PART II.

CHAPTER I.

THE seeds that they planted on the grave of Joy's mother had grown into flowers, and the first pang of parting was over. Twok had been a member of Dr. Somerville's family ever since the death of Mrs. Cougles, and when Joy called one day to see the doctor, she invited him into the parlor to have a chat with her, as the doctor was not at home.

"You must be very lonely working there in the shop without anybody," said Twok.

"I am lonely."

"It seems selfish for me to stay here with everything so pleasant while you are there alone, but Mrs. Somerville said it would not be proper for me to live there after your mother was gone. I will be able to go to see you often after you marry Mary. It will be very soon now; will it not? I have something I want to give to you. It is the money you gave me for music lessons. It wasn't fair for me to take it, and I will not feel happy unless you let me pay it back. I can never repay you for bringing me up, and being both father and brother to me, but I will never forget your kindness."

Twok took from her pocket a roll of bills and nervously shoved them into Joy's hand, saying,

"I earned it all myself. I'll tell you how next time I see you. Here is Dr. Somerville now. I'll leave you to him."

Twok retired to the library, and seating herself in a recess of the large bay-window, where she was concealed by the curtains, gazed outdoors at nothing, with the old thought in her mind that life was nothing better than a dream. Her dream took this shape just then. Dr. Somerville and Joy, whom she had left in the parlor, seemed to be in the library close to her, talking. The doctor said,

"Well, why don't you marry Mary?"

"Marry Mary?"

"Yes. That is what I said. What do you mean by this mystery and this nonsense? You never told me, although I have confided in you as if you were my own son. You don't even tell her father, and I would never have known but for that innocent child Twok, who thought that of course you would have told me."

Now if Twok had not been dreaming she would have come forward, excused herself and left the room, but people in dreams cannot control their actions, and so she sat still and listened.

"I am too poor to get married."

"You are no poorer than Mary's father was when he married. Besides you are richer than you think. Years ago, on your twelfth birthday, I put into the bank a sum of money, which has amounted with interest to two thousand dollars, intending to give it to you when you married to please me. Now I always liked Mary, and I won't hold back because you were mean enough not to confide in me. Then although I dislike old man Slemmings, I know how to manage him. You just go and settle on the day with Mary, and I will break the news gently to her father and make him agree to settle two thousand dollars on her at once. With four thousand dollars, and what you can get for your house and shop, you can start a small foundry either here or in Hamilton, and I'll undertake to say that you will be a rich man within ten years. All the rich foundry-men in Hamilton began with very little, and some of them are very wealthy now. Give me your hand, my boy."

"Doctor, I'm ever so much obliged for your kind offer, but I can't do it."

"What do you mean by it? Ain't you engaged to the girl?"

"Yes."

"Then why won't you marry her?"

"Because I love Twok."

Dr. Somerville, who had been nervously handling a book which lay on the table beside him, took it up angrily and threw it at Joy's head. It missed its mark, and passing between the curtains fell at Twok's feet.

"Confound you!" said he, "you are giving me a temper as bad as you had yourself when I first knew you. You are an infamous brute, and I have been deceived all my life."

"Let me tell my story. I must confess the whole, now that I have told part. You know I was always fond of theorizing. One of my pet theories was, that there wasn't such a thing as love between the sexes as distinct from that love which a man has for any good woman. It is only concentration, I said to myself. All men have a natural liking for women, and a man can concentrate this feeling upon one woman when he has a mind. It will develope itself in time, until he grows to love her better than anyone else. The only woman that I loved in those days was mother, but I always liked Mary from the time she was a pretty little girl as much as I disliked her brother Sam. As I grew older the thought sometimes crossed my mind that I might decide to fall in love with her, or, in other words, make her the object of my concentrated liking for woman. Still I scarcely ever thought of her when I was at work, and never while reading or studying. But one Sunday I found her in trouble. Sam, confound the brute, had been misusing her, and she was crying in the ravine. I found what was the matter, and said, 'I wish I were your brother, Mary, instead of Sam. All your love would not be thrown away then, for I would love back.' She answered, 'I wish you were.' Then I said, 'Mary, you can't be my sister, but you can be my wife some day. Will you?' And she said, 'yes.' We decided on the way up to the house, that we would wait five years. By that time I thought I would have so concentrated my affection as to love her devotedly. I told my mother at once, and Mary said she would tell her mother, but begged me not to tell her father or Sam, for they would tease her to death about it. I did not make any effort at concentration for some time, as I thought there was lots of time in five years. I did not pay any attention to other girls, but wasted no time in lovemaking, and seldom thought of her. When my work was done, it was a relief sometimes to walk home with her, and I enjoyed it. She soon ceased coming to help us with the work, and after that I saw little of her, except when we met at church or some such place, when I usually walked home with her. Twok and I were as brother and sister. Before going to bed she always kissed both mother and me good-night, but one night about a year after my engagement began she omitted to kiss me. I had grown so accustomed to it that something seemed missing without it, and when she neglected me a second time on the following evening, I said, 'Why don't you kiss me, too, when you kiss mother?' She looked at me very gravely, and said in a quite determined little way that she has, 'I don't think it is proper for girls to kiss anybody except the persons whom they are going to marry.' 'Not even their brothers?' said I smiling. 'Yes,' she said; 'but you are not exactly my brother, although you have been just as good as one.' I said nothing more, but was much amused, thinking she had got the idea from some book. She never kissed me again, and I missed that good-night kiss greatly. It was not very long afterward that Sam stole a kiss, and got his face scarred for his impudence. I hated him for it. She was only about twelve years old then, I fancy, and I was not exactly in love yet, but she grew very rapidly after that, and was soon as large as she is now, which is not very big. She felt so sorry for having scarred Sam that she got over her dislike for him, and he was so evidently infatuated with her, that I began to fear that she would marry him when she grew older. The thought was torture to me, for it always seemed to me that his liking for her was as brutal as himself. A variety of passions go under the name of love. Some of them are merely animal in their character and are little better than lust; others are pure, but none of them exactly correspond with the love a man has for his mother. Our language is wanting in a word to express the commonest passion. We are ready enough to find new names for new things, but we cannot give a new name to such an old thing as that. Love is beautifully described under the name of charity in I. Corinthians, xiii. chapter. The passion which a man has for a woman is a different thing from that. It isn't love. Love doesn't always go with it, and that is why many marriages are unhappy. To make a true marriage, love and this feeling must unite. This feeling is so different from love, that hate sometimes springs from it, and yet it is akin to love, and if it is not strengthened and purified by love, it will not be enduring. Well, I thought about Twok while I worked and while I walked and while I read and while I talked to other people about other things, until the thought of her became a part of myself. It was most curious, too, that when reading a novel I always found myself putting Twok into the place of the heroine. Reading a novel became to me like watching a play, with Twok in the leading role. The old novels being re-read with her as the actress took on a new meaning. It mattered not whether the heroine as described in the book resembled Twok; it was always Twok's face that filled the book. When the heroine said this or that, it was always with Twok's expression and Twok's tone of voice. She has so many expressions and so many tones. There seems to be a different one for every emotion of the mind, and I remember them all distinctly and know the meaning of most of them. When I thought of all this I could not but know that I was in love with Twok, and was often startled to find my hammer pounding out the words, ' Twok, I love you.' This would happen even when I was thinking of something else, for other thoughts seldom so engrossed my attention as to crowd her out of my mind for a moment. It may be hard for you to believe this to be strictly true. I could not have believed it had I not experienced it. In fact, I used to believe it was impossible to think of two things at once. Perhaps I only felt about her while I thought about other things."

"Fudge!" said Dr. Somerville, interrupting. "You are merely fascinated by the girl's beauty. She'll lose that in great part as she grows older, and then you'll come to your senses."

"No, it isn't that, for strange as it may seem after all these years that I have known her, I scarcely know what her features are like. I could draw a picture of Mary easily, for I know the exact shape of her forehead and nose and mouth and chin, but I couldn't draw a picture bearing the slightest resemblance to Twok. Sometimes I fancy that it is Twok's spirit instead of her body that I see when I look at her, for while she seems real enough at the time, when she is gone there is the same indefinite impression of face and figure that a vision of a spirit would leave. I often think that I will look at her closely the next time and see what her features are like, but the result is always the same."

"Well, so far as expressions go, she appears the same to other people. She has what is called a mobile face and the expression is always changing in conformation to her many sided character, shaping itself to her spirit, I suppose. If she should ever grow to be wicked, I believe she would become positively ugly. It is her goodness that makes her lovely. Don't imagine yourself in love because you see what everybody else sees. You have a large imagination and exaggerate it somewhat. That is all."

"Well, what am I to do?"

"Marry Mary, of course, you brute! You can't desert the girl after such a long engagement. I am ashamed of you. Have you ever said anything to her?"

"No, I could not bear to hurt her feelings. I know it was cowardly, but I thought that after she had been at the college for a while she would get used to fashionable notions, and would not like the idea of being a blacksmith's wife, and that by waiting awhile the news would not be very disagreeable to her, because she would have lots of better chances."

"If you looked like a common blacksmith, there would have been some reason in supposing that association with stylish people would make her ashamed of you; but when you are not at your work you might be mistaken for a member of your father's profession, were it not that your hands have been hardened and blackened by your work as lawyer's ink could never have made them."

"Then," continued Joy, "there was a struggle in my mind regarding whether or not it was my duty to marry her unless she herself wished to break it off."

"Joy, you must conquer this passion for Twok. I used to call you my ideal boy, but you will fall very far from my idea of an ideal man if you cannot conquer this. What have you ever had to contend against? You were born moral. It was never any temptation to you to lie or steal. You were by nature gentle, and cruelty, which is a source of gratification to some men, is revolting to you. Is that anything to be proud of? Not a bit of it. You were born that way. Some men can't bear to be ridiculed. They hate to be laughed at, and so are tempted to evil doing which they would else avoid; but if you knew a thing was wrong you couldn't be laughed into doing it simply because you had a natural contempt for ridicule. Then you had a good pure mother and were blessed with a healthy body and a strong mind. The little evils that entrap other men are no temptation to you, and the only things you have ever had to conquer were your own bad temper, your hatred for Sam and this absurd passion for Twok. The first you did conquer; of the second I am not so sure, but think you conquered that, too; you are allowing the last to gain complete control over you without any effort to resist. Joy, I'm ashamed of you. You whom I admired and imitated, boy as you were, for years, have sadly disappointed me. I tell you that Sam Slemmings has done more to be proud of than you have. He had naturally low and brutal impulses, but he is making a man of himself. He did not care for study, but forced himself to study in order that he might have a place in the world. The very things that you do with pleasure he does with an effort, and so is always growing better able to conquer himself. If you both go on in the same way to the end he will be the finer man of the two. If you with your noble nature will resist every temptation that comes to you, you will be an ideal man. If not, you had better never have been born. I sometimes think that after death, on the threshold of the life eternal there will be some one awful temptation to which we all must come. Those who have grown strong in character, in resisting the temptations of this life, be they little or big, will pass through that trial triumphantly. Those who have failed here will fail there. If you yield to this temptation; if you fail to conquer yourself now, how can you expect to do it then? But, my boy, you will not disappoint me. You must conquer."

There was a ring at the door bell. Someone wished to see Dr. Somerville, and both men left the room and the house. Twok heard the front door slam behind them and saw them walk away in opposite directions. Taking up the book that had fallen at her feet, she replaced it on the table. She was very cold although the day was hot, and as she walked up stairs to her room, she shivered as if with the ague. But arrived there, a flush came into her face, and with a very determined expression she put a few articles in a satchel, wrote a little note, addressed it to the doctor, and then satchel in hand went down stairs and out of the house. Her brain was busy thinking of what she had heard. Her strongest feeling was, that she must go some place where Joy could not find her. So Joy loved her instead of Mary. That was what the hammer was saying all the time. It was very mean of him to desert Mary, but perhaps he could not help it. Certainly Mary did not understand his character or his ideas as well as she did. Why, Mary never knew that he made his hammer talk. Poor fellow! He lost everything he loved. First Sam poisoned his dog, Lion; then his mother died; and now, she was running away from him. But after being engaged to Mary he had no right to fall in love with anyone else. If she were out of the way, he would soon go back to Mary and marry her. Then everybody would be happy, except—except Twok. She could not be very happy, for, she said to herself softly, " If you know that you are loved, you can't help loving back." Perhaps if she remained away long enough he would stop loving her, and then she could go back and listen to the talking hammer. But if he stopped loving her he wouldn't hammer her name any more, and what was the use of listening to his hammer repeating Greek verbs and enunciations in Euclid? No, she would never come back. Everybody said she was pretty, and she could sing and dance and had been called a good reader: why should she not be an actress?

As these thoughts passed through Twok's mind she walked rapidly toward the ravine, and following one of the many steep paths leading into it, soon stood before the door of Carlock's ivy-covered hut. The old man answered her knock, beckoned her to enter and led her to his cave, saying as he did so,

"You may have come to see me often for all I know. I can never hear anyone knocking when I'm down in my cave."

"This is only the second time I have come."

"And what brings you here this time after neglecting me so long?" he said as they reached the cave.

"You told me not to come often," she replied, "and wished me to keep your secret. If I had come, it might have been hard to have kept it, as people would ask questions."

"Yes. But why have you come now?"

"Are you sorry to see me?"

"No. I am very glad to see you, but I like people to answer my questions. Why have you come now?"

"Because I'm running away."

"Jupiter! Have they been ill-treating you?"

"No. They have been very kind to me. But I have kept your secret all these years without asking any questions. Can you not keep mine and help me to get away where no one can find me without asking me any questions?"

"Most assuredly. See. I have prepared this especially for you. I have for years had a fancy that you would sometime come to me in trouble, and with that in view have fitted this room for you."

He advanced to a corner of the cave which he had partitioned off from the rest, and throwing open a door invited her to enter. She had never seen a room so handsomely furnished. The walls and ceiling were covered with costly and tasteful paper. There were lovely paintings on the walls, a soft velvet carpet on the floor and a beautiful rosewood bedroom set. The room was lighted by two gas jets.

"This is your own room," the old man said "I have been working at it at intervals ever since you called to see me when you were a little girl. You may stay here as long as you like and I will provide you with every luxury, and just so soon as you wish I will assist you to escape."

"I don't think it would be wise for me to stay here. You could surely help me to escape at once. It was so very kind of you to plan the room for me that I am ashamed to refuse to occupy it, but—but I don't think it would be discreet."

"It is utterly impossible for me to help you at once. I am obliged to be away for several days. Was just getting ready to leave when you came. Stay here and amuse yourself for a few days. I have lots of books. You need not be lonely if you are left alone, and there is lots to eat. No one will find you here, and you can better elude pursuit after several days have passed. I will see that everything is right. Can't you trust me?"

"Yes, I suppose so," said Twok, doubtfully.

She took the chair which he offered her and watched him making hurried preparations for departure. He stopped now and then to speak to her. What did she propose to do, he asked. What were her plans? Twok said she hardly knew what her plans were. She had thought of being an actress, but was undecided. All she knew now was, that she must go somewhere far from Linklater. Then old Carlock said that he had been something of an actor himself when he was— well in the days when he was fat. And now, he didn't mind telling her that he was going to New York very soon on secret business, and if she liked to go with him he would disguise both himself and her so that no one could recognize them. She should pass as his grand-daughter, and he would not leave her until she had secured a place with a respectable theatrical company. In the meantime, she must manage to amuse herself during his absence. He showed her how to use the gas and opened one of the big blue boxes, saying it was full of books and he was sure she would find them interesting. Some of them were books of adventure; others recorded the narrow escapes of robbers, smugglers and fences, or described the work of detectives; but some of them were love stories. Now for his own part, he said, he was too old to love, but a man was never too old to enjoy love stories, and he knew a pretty girl like her couldn't help liking them. With this parting information the garrulous old man, who had been silent so long, took his departure. As he shut the door after him, Twok heard the click of the lock, and the thought flashed upon her that she was a prisoner until he chose to release her. She climbed up the ladder and tried the door. It was securely locked, and she had no key. Suppose the old man should never come back. He might take a notion to leave her there. To be sure he seemed to like her, or else he would not have prepared for her such a lovely room; but then he might be killed, or most probable of all he might be arrested and put in jail on account of his strange habits. In any case, if he should not come back within a few days, she would starve to death. Why had she not asked him for a key? But it was just like the simpleton she was to run away from Joy, who loved her so, and trust herself to a dishonest old knife-maker, who had skin enough for two ordinary men ; and Twok concluded by saying aloud, " If you do starve to death, you silly girl, it will be your own fault and it will serve you right."

Having administered this rebuke to herself and given a stray lock of hair a very hard pull by way of punishment, she undressed and went to bed without having eaten anything ; she did not sleep, however, but lay awake nearly all night, wondering what Joy would do without her and what the future had in store for her.

CHAPTER II.

AS Joy walked home after his interview with Dr. Somerville, he determined to call on Mary Slemmings that evening and tell her the state of his mind. He ate his supper in solitude and walked to the house of Mr. Slemmings by the most roundabout way. Arrived there, he hesitated and almost decided to return, but screwing up his courage knocked at the door, which being opened by one of the younger children, he asked for Mary. She was not at home, he was told, having left the day before on a visit to some of her college friends who had graduated at the same time as herself. He walked home with a sense of relief, having honorably attempted to perform a disagreeable duty. Alvin Linklater was waiting for him at the shop.

"I want to ask you some questions, Joy," said he. "Since I talked with you about God one day a long time ago I have thought much of what you said and am half inclined to think you are right. I certainly would be happier believing in God. But how is it that so many scientists are infidels?"

"All scientists are not infidels, but so-called science is as yet only on the threshold of knowledge, and some students of science are blinded to the truth by what little they know. Bacon says, 'A little philosophy inclineth man's mind to atheism, but depth of philosophy bringeth men's minds about to religion; for while the mind of man looketh upon second causes scattered, it may rest in them and go no further; but when it holdeth the chain of them confederate and linked together it must needs turn to Providence and Deity.' I think Bacon was right. Nearly all the great scientists believe in some sort of a God, and although many of them do not believe in the inspiration of the Bible, there are a few who even go so far as that. Now, Alvin, a mistake commonly made among all classes is taking the material and the plan for the designer, and the instrument for the agent. In our association with our friends we are much influenced by their personal appearance, and much of our affection often arises from admiration for beauty in form or feature; and this to a certain extent is right, for the personal appearance is generally some indication of the character and disposition. But this substitution of the material for the spiritual, this taking of the external appearance for the internal cause, is often carried too far. When a friend dies we weep over the senseless clay which he once animated, and although most of us, perhaps, only look at the body as a cast-off garment dear to us from association with our friend, yet there are many who consider it not as the garment, but as the being, and mourn their dead friend as lost forever. So in the study of nature, some men look upon the various phenomena and peculiar adjustments not as evidences of an almighty mind and grand purpose, but as the mere outcome of senseless matter, and like Professor Tyndall regard matter as that mysterious thing by which all these matchless contrivances and wonderful results are accomplished. In comparing the works of ancient and modern writers one can scarcely fail to be struck by the contrast between their respective views of nature. To the Greek and the Roman, matter was inanimate and inert; all the motions and phenomena of nature were caused and controlled by spiritual agents. There was Zeus with his thunderbolts, the collector of the black clouds, the hurler of the white lightning, who sent rain to refresh the earth; Posidon, the god of the sea, and Æolus, the father of the winds, and not only were the grand and striking features of nature thus deified, but each little stream or fountain had its tutelar god or goddess, and all the movements of matter were ascribed to divine influences. But having satisfied themselves as to the agent of action, the ancients troubled themselves little about the mode of operation.

Modern investigators of nature, on the other hand, seem to be so deeply absorbed in searching for and examining into the mode of action that they almost lose sight of the agent. They find that lightning results from the contact of clouds charged with opposite electricities, and that thunder is occasioned by the vibrations of the air, as it collapses and seeks to restore its own equilibrium, and then they laugh at the ancients for supposing that these phenomena were produced by Zeus. But in reality they have not shown that Zeus does not produce them; they have only found how he performs the operation. They are guided in their searches for the "how" of nature by the more easily discovered "why" of nature, and in thus making use of the "why" of nature are forced to acknowledge the prevalence of design; and yet, strange to say, many of them do not believe in the existence of the great Designer. Even believers in God and the Bible seem to look at the relation between God and nature from an entirely wrong standpoint, for although we have been taught that God is everywhere, we do not fully realize the great fact, but are accustomed to regard Him as a far-away being, and in addressing Him or speaking of Him often raise our eyes as if the great being whom we supplicate were somewhere in the skies. Perhaps you have read what Pope says in this regard:

> 'All are but parts of one stupendous whole
> Whose body Nature is, and God the Soul;
> That changed through all and yet in all the same;
> Great in the earth as in the ethereal frame;
> Warms in the sun, refreshes in the breeze;
> Glows in the stars, and blossoms in the trees;
> Lives through all life, extends through all extent,
> Spreads undivided, operates unspent;
> Breathes in our soul, informs our mortal part
> As full as perfect in a hair as heart;
> As full as perfect in vile man that mourns
> As the wrapt seraph that adores and burns;
> To Him no high, no low, no great, no small—
> He fills, He bounds, connects and equals all.'

"But Pope was not the first to originate the idea. It is as old as the ages. St. Paul, speaking to the men of Athens of the Unknown God, said, 'In Him we live and move and have our being;' and the Roman poet Virgil seems to have had some glimmering of the truth, for he made the shade of Anchises say in reply to Æneas: 'In the first place the spirit within nourishes the heavens, the earth and the watery plains, the shining orb of the moon and the Titanian stars; and the mind diffused through all the limbs actuates the mass and mingles with the vast body. Thence the race of men and beasts, the vital principles of the flying kind and the monsters which the ocean breeds under its smooth plain.'

"So you see Pope's idea is exactly the same as Virgil's and St. Paul's, only differently expressed. I don't mean to say that he stole it from Virgil. Indeed I was vain enough to think the idea originated with me and wrote an essay on it, but afterward read these and other passages and found that the idea had been expressed ages before I was born. The idea was very familiar to the ancient philosophers, but I cannot quote any other passages just at present."

"Why, you are a sort of Pantheist," said Alvin.

"Something like that. God has control of the universe of matter, just as man has control of a small portion of matter called his body; and just as man, by the action of his will, can cause the instant motion of his legs; so God said, 'Let there be light: and there was light.'"

"It is a grand idea, Joy, but it wasn't altogether to talk about this that I came. I wanted to tell you something. I believe I am falling in love with Twok."

"Everybody seems to fall in love with her," said Joy, moodily.

"You see," continued Alvin, "she has such a queer face. It is never the same for more than a few minutes at a time. A fellow can't help thinking about it."

"Do you think about her all the time?"

"No. It isn't as bad as that, but I think about her more

than of any other girl. I don't know that I am in love. In fact, the feeling I have for her is more like the interest one takes in the heroine of a novel, only intensified. I can't help thinking about her, and I am very curious to know something of her past. Now, you have never made any effort to discover Twok's parentage. She is so lovely and ladylike that she must have come of good parents. Couldn't we hunt them up?"

"Twok always seemed to think that her father and mother died when she was a baby, and that her grandfather, an old basket maker, took care of her until he died, too, after which, she lived with an old woman named Meg until she ran away and came here."

"I can't help thinking about my dream. Might it not be possible that she is the child of my lost aunt? But here is Dr. Somerville. I will see you to-morrow, and talk it over. Good night. How are you, doctor?"

As Alvin left the shop Dr. Somerville entered.

"You are a *fine* fellow," he said, ironically, as he took a seat.

"Yes?" said Joy. "What is the trouble now?"

"Trouble enough. You have driven Twok away. Read that."

Joy took with trembling hand a note, which read:

DEAR DR. SOMERVILLE:

I heard you and Joy talking in the library. I was in the window, and thought it was a dream at first, for I was half dosing, and had left you both in the parlor a moment before. Afterward I was ashamed to come out. I will write to you sometimes but you must not try to find me until Joy is married. I will never forget how kind you and Mrs. Somerville have been, or what Joy has done for me; he was both father and brother to me. You must comfort him, and don't be cross to him, please.

Yours very sincerely,

TWOK.

CHAPTER III.

JOY is in his forge. Not hammering the iron or reading a book, but only looking at the fire. We look at the fire, too. It is not burning very brightly now, hardly brightly enough to show us Joy's face as he looks at it. He ought to put on more coal and blow the bellows, but he does not seem to know that the fire is low. Perhaps he sees something else there which shuts out from his vision the low burning fire and the darkening room. Let us look over his shoulder and see for ourselves. We see nothing but the fire sinking down into the ashes, and the iron that will soon grow cold if Joy does not arouse from his reverie. Could we get a look at his brain we might see what Joy sees, for assuredly he is looking at something. And now we are looking at it; and what do we see? Ah! there is a face there, the face of a child that is fast merging into that of a woman—a pleasant, cheery face to look at, more cheery than Joy's own. Have we ever seen it before? Call to mind a child living in one of the lowest haunts among the canals of Buffalo, a child fleeing in fright from an imaginary monster that she called Law; a child struggling to escape from Sam Slemmings—Joy sees it too and frowns—a moment after escaping from him with a grateful look at—why, at Joy himself. Call these to mind and you have pictured to yourself the face that Joy is looking at: a sweet face, a kindly, loving, lovely face; a charming face. It is no wonder that Joy has looked at it with all its changing expressions; looked at it as child, maiden, middle aged woman and grey haired old lady, for Joy is looking at the future as well as at the past, and the face will change somewhat with time; looked at it until the fire has gradually burned down into the ashes and the room has grown dark ; looked at it all unconscious of another face that has been looking at him all the time. If Joy could see this other face it would startle him out of his reverie. A strong, determined, strikingly handsome face, framed in an almost perfect beard of black streaked with grey ; the face of a man with a purpose that has worn itself into his character. This face belongs to a tall, well formed, stylishly dressed man who at last steps forward and says,

"What have you done with my child ?"

Joy looks up startled, but not surprised. So this is her father. Yes, he does not look much like Twok, but Joy has seen an expression something like his on her face at times. So he answers in a dazed sort of way, "She has run away."

"Young man, I have been looking at you for a long time. I like your face. We must have no secrets. I am sure she is my lost daughter because she bears the name I gave her. Some men have identified their lost children by scars or marks on the body. I can identify my child by her name. Tell me what you know and I will tell you the story of my life, which no one has ever heard. I feel somehow as if you could sympathize with me. I have never before met anyone in whom I could confide."

Joy briefly and sadly tells what he knows about Twok up to the time of his mother's death, not omitting to mention Alvin's dream and all the circumstances connected with it.

"Yes," says the stranger. "I can understand that. I have a strange faculty. I do not know whether anyone else possesses it or not. It is something akin to mind-reading. It is a well known fact that there are men who have developed the faculty of mind reading to an extraordinary degree. I have not that faculty, but I have another that may be common enough for all I know, but I have never met a man who possessed it. By standing over a sleeping person and looking at him intently I can imprint images upon his brain, and what is perhaps more extraordinary, I have that faculty under control. ·I stood over that boy as he slept under the elm tree in the moonlight. I was the young man of his dream and took a notion to let him see the thing as it happened. You start from me. Hear all first. Then you will condemn, but pity, too. My name is Trenwith."

"Twok Trenwith," murmurs Joy.

"Yes, that is her name. That is what I called her. My own is Jasper Trenwith. I was born in Montreal. My father was an American, a refugee from justice. He had gone into counterfeiting on a very extensive scale and made a large fortune out of it. They never found him out, but he was a clever man and knew just how far to go. When he could safely go no further, he went out of the business and moved to Canada to live on the fortune he had made with his fingers. I don't mean that he took the queer money to Canada with him. He had exchanged it for good, honest gold before he went out of the business. Ah, he was a clever man."

"That was Twok's grandfather?"

"Yes, but you needn't blame her for his crimes or those of her father either."

"I will not. She is honest and pure and unselfish. What do I care for her grandfather?"

"Yes. She is like her mother and my mother. The women of our family were always very good. I have heard my father say so. But her grandfather wasn't such a bad fellow either. His crime was rather the result of a misconception than of a determination to do wrong. To be sure he had not enough confidence in the rightfulness of it to confide in my mother. It would have killed her had she known. I think myself that anything that a man is afraid to confide to his wife or his mother must be wrong. But the way he explained it sounded plausible enough to me then, although you who are a thinker will see the fallacy of it. He certainly was a kind-hearted man, as tender as a woman with my mother and always ready not only to relieve distress with his ill-gotten money, but to suffer himself for others. I have known him to give his overcoat and warm gloves to a poor wretch whom we met on a cold winter night when the thermometer was below zero, and then walk to our home a mile away without the warm things to which he was accustomed. I don't mean to defend counterfeiting, but I must say that many a speculator in stocks, whom no one would think of calling dishonest, is more guilty than was he. Well, one day when I was about fifteen years old my father said to me, ' Jasper, you are a smart boy. I don't mind confiding in you. This country is too slow for me.'

" ' Are you going to move to the States ? ' I asked.

" ' No, no, boy,' he replied. ' I will make things move myself. The wheels of industry are clogged for want of money. We will make things lively. We'll set trade abooming. This country has great resources. The Canadians will be a great people some day. All they want is money to develop the resources. We will supply the money, Jasper. Labor ought to be the source of money, but owing to the wrong ideas of the men who govern us, money is the source of labor. There are thousands of men out of work, not because there is no work to be done, but because there is no money to pay for the work. We have vast areas of farm lands and almost limitless mineral deposits ; we want canals and wagon roads and railways. Everywhere we have undeveloped wealth and unimproved sources of labor. And yet there are thousands of men standing idle, not because they don't want to work, but because there is no money to pay for their labor ; and so all the vast resources of this great country must remain undeveloped unless someone supplies the money. We will make money, my boy, and watch the wheels of industry spin.'

" 'You don't mean counterfeiting?' I said, in astonishment.

" ' Call it so if you please,' he replied. ' There's no harm in counterfeiting if it isn't bungled. A bungler has no right to be a counterfeiter. The business requires extraordinary skill of eye and hand, accompanied by keen judgment, a thorough knowledge of business and of men, and temperate habits. If you bungle the business you are apt to get into trouble yourself, or, what is worse, get innocent people into trouble. Clever counterfeiting only increases the money of the country, and so helps trade and production. But an honest counterfeiter will in the first place be sure that his work is so well done that the difference between the counterfeit and the real cannot be easily detected, and in the second place he must be careful in circulating the money that in case of discovery suspicion cannot fall on honest people. There is no harm in making a tool of a rogue or casting suspicion on him. If he is arrested and sent to jail, so much the better for the community at large. But never confide in a rogue. Let him suppose that he is cheating you, and disguise yourself in dealing with him so that he cannot afterward recognize you. A successful counterfeiter must be a born actor. I think you have the necessary talents if you will patiently cultivate them under my direction.'

"Now I do not know whether my father believed all this or not. He may have fully believed it, for he certainly did not need to resort to counterfeiting in Canada in order to secure money for his own use, as he already had a large fortune and was not by any means extravagant in his mode of living. Either he must have believed it or else there must be a sort of fascination in the business after one has learned it. Anyhow I believed it then and admired my father's wonderful skill and ingenuity when he showed me all his appliances, and after binding me to secrecy explained how he had carried on operations in the United States. I felt highly honored by my father's confidence in me and determined to become as skilful as he was. The only thing I disliked about it was that I could not mention it to my mother, from whom I had never before had a secret. We were to begin work next day in a room which my father always kept locked.

He went out for a ride that afternoon and was brought home crushed and dead before night. His horse had thrown him."

"My father died in much the same way," says Joy, interrupting the stranger. "He had been drinking."

"My father," says Trenwith, proudly, "had not been drinking. He never tasted liquor in his life, and I never have myself. Almost stunned with grief, as I was, my first thought was; 'It must not be known that he was a counterfeiter.' Throwing myself on his prostrate body in a well sembled passion of grief, I deftly thrust my hand into his pocket, and taking from it the key with which he locked the door of his secret room transferred it to my own pocket. The doctor and the policeman who came with the body saw nothing but a boy weeping over his father's corpse. But the tears were forced. The whole scene was a piece of acting. I loved my father, but I am not demonstrative by nature, and that was not the way I would naturally have expressed my grief. For the time being, the desire to protect his memory and prevent the confiscation of his property, upon which my mother and baby sister as well as myself depended, crowded out all other thoughts. Although my father had never counterfeited in Canada, I feared that if his tools were discovered by the authorities, everything would be seized. So when they left us alone, I excused myself as soon as possible to my mother, and hastening to the secret room destroyed all evidences of my father's profession. Notwithstanding my admiration for my father at that time, I did think he had acted very foolishly in placing nothing but a curiously constructed lock and key between the public and his secret. I had no inclination to continue the business on my own account. I had been impressed with the idea that to counterfeit successfully, so as not to endanger one's self or injure other people, required extraordinary ability, and I was satisfied that without my father to instruct me I could never succeed. My mother had no difficulty in securing the fortune he had left us. It amounted to one hundred thousand dollars, and according to his will half of it was to become mine when I attained my majority. So I had a tutor and my mother herself taught my little sister, and we all lived very happily together until a few months after I was twenty-one. Then my little sister was taken ill with that terrible disease, small-pox, and died. I think I carried it to her in my clothes, for I had foolishly visited a poor family who were sick with it. Mother and I nursed the child until she died and neither of us took the disease. The doctor in attendance advised us to take a change of air at once and we accordingly journeyed by steamer to Hamilton, where my mother was prostrated with brain fever. For days I watched over her despairingly. At last she grew better and regained consciousness, but seemed to have forgotten all about Nellie's death and constantly asked for her. I put her off from day to day by evasive answers, and one day took a long drive into the country, leaving her in charge of a nurse. I thought a quiet drive would do me good and help me to determine the best way to explain to her that Nellie was dead. I drove to Linklater estate. There was a fine view from the hill and while I was looking at it with the eye of an artist, for I was something of a painter, I heard someone call, 'Nellie, keep your hat on," and a child almost exactly the size of my dead sister and with hair of the same color ran down the path toward the old elm under which Alvin Linklater slept many years afterward. I followed and watched her as she disobediently took off her hat and began to fill it with dandelions, which grew in profusion around.

"She was not like my sister, being much prettier; but as I watched her I thought, 'My mother does not remember anything about Nellie's sickness and death. Perhaps she also forgets what she looked like. I will take this child to her and perhaps she will think it is our Nellie.' So I clasped the child in my arms and ran with her to my carriage, which was waiting for me a little distance down the road where I had tied the horse. It was a mad, unreasoning, wicked thing to do, but my mind was in a state of unusual excitement for I had nursed both Nellie and mother during their illness and was almost on the verge of brain fever from the effects of the strain and anxiety for my mother. The child was much alarmed at first but I told her I was going to take her for a nice drive, and that I would buy her a doll almost as big as herself. She was greatly pleased then and said,

"'Oh, will you buy me a baby doll? I would so like a baby doll. They always buy me grown-up dolls, with their hair done up like mamma's. Little girls don't like to nurse grown-up dolls. They want to nurse baby dolls.'

"I promised to get her a baby doll as soon as we reached Hamilton and in the meantime gave her some candies which I had in my pocket. On reaching Hamilton I drove at once to the house we occupied, and leaving Nellie with the nurse started to buy a baby doll. I went to every store in the place, which was only a village at that time, but could not find a baby doll. Returning I told Nellie I could not find a baby doll in Hamilton but that we would take the boat for Toronto, where we would be sure to find one. Then Nellie began to cry and asked me to take her home, but I pacified her and we started for Toronto by boat that evening. I put the child in mother's arms as we started, saying, 'Mother, here is Nellie.' It was growing dark and mother clasped the child in her arms without scanning her features, and Nellie, although she sobbed in a heartbroken way for a little while, did not try to escape from my mother's arms and after a time fell asleep. When mother saw her in the light she became much excited and said, 'This is not my Nellie.' When we reached Toronto, mother was quite ill again. We went to the leading hotel, and after making every arrangement for mother's comfort I went out to buy a baby doll for Nellie. I visited all the stores where there seemed to be any possibility of finding dolls and made a number of purchases, including miniature furniture and a doll's tea set. There were men and women, old, young and middle aged, in that doll world, and I even found some little boys and girls, but there wasn't a single baby doll to be found. So at last in despair I bought half a dozen grown-up dolls and started off with the determination to convert one of them into a baby. Surely, I said to myself, if I am fitted to be a successful counterfeiter, as my father thought, I ought to be able to manufacture a baby out of one of these wax ladies. Just then I noticed in the window of a millinery establishment a real baby doll almost life sized, which was used for the purpose of displaying pretty baby dresses. In a moment I was bargaining with the milliner for the doll, dresses and all, and having with some difficulty induced her to sell it returned to the hotel, only to find that my mother was worse. She had a relapse, and in spite of the most careful nursing died in a few days. During the days before my mother died my time was divided between her and Nellie. The child was still anxious to go home, but when I told her that she was visiting me and that I could not take her home until my mother got well, she became more contented. She was so delighted with her baby doll that she paid no attention to the other playthings, merely looking at them for a moment and then putting them aside to take possession of her baby again. The mother's instinct is strong in nearly all girls; and I have never since seen a little girl nursing a doll that looked old enough to be her mother without thinking of Nellie's words, 'Little girls don't like to nurse grown-up dolls; they want to nurse baby dolls.' Buy for a child a fashionable young lady doll arrayed in her wedding dress and with her hair banged in the latest style, and if that doll could talk she would make indignant protest against the way in which the child treats her. 'Goodness gracious!' she would exclaim; 'that child is mussing my hair and spoiling my dress and hugging me and talking to me as if I were a one-year-old baby.' Yes, the motherly instinct is usually strong in the little girls that grow into motherly women. But to return to my story.

You can imagine my feelings when my mother died and I was left alone in the world. What I had done in kindness, hoping to hasten her recovery, had brought on a relapse causing her death. I had the body taken to Montreal for burial. Nellie accompanied me on the boat. She asked me often when I would take her home, and sometimes seemed to be very homesick, but I treated her so kindly and gave her such pretty toys to play with and such dainties to eat, that she could not fail to like me. What I would do with her I did not try to determine, but put the thought away, only saying to myself, 'I can't give her up yet ; I have no one else.' On the way to Montreal she did not seem to be at all well, and when I sent for a doctor on arriving in the city, he said she had typhoid fever. I told him and all my friends that she was an orphan whom my mother had adopted in the west before her death, and of course everyone sympathized with me in my great affliction. I watched over that child almost night and day with guilty feelings of remorse, often saying to myself, 'If she lives, I will take her home ; if she dies, I will kill myself as a murderer who has no right to live, and can take no comfort in life.' She did live, but the fever had almost blotted out her recollection of the past. Then came my temptation. I said to myself, 'The worst of her parents' grief for her loss must now be over. They must suppose her dead. She herself hardly remembers the past, and is learning to love me. My wealth will enable me to give her advantages that she could not have at home. Her parents no doubt have or will have other children, while I have no relation.' All this was supremely selfish. I have since learned what it is for a parent to lose a child, and had I known then, it would have been very different. Selfishness overcame my sense of right, and I told my friends that my mother's adopted child would be my sister, and share my wealth. Then an idea which struck me gradually grew into a fixed purpose. I would educate this girl to be my wife. That she might not regard me as a brother I placed her with a lady whom I paid liberally for educating her, making occasional visits myself to see how she was progressing. I have said that I never drank. I was temperate in all respects, living a life of the strictest chastity, and patiently waiting until Nellie should be old enough to marry me. Once I visited this village and found to my relief that her parents were both dead. Then I felt that no one had a stronger claim upon her than myself. I will not weary you with the story of my lovemaking. If you have been in love, you understand it all. If not, it would be useless to try to explain it. One has theories about love before it comes to himself, but they are all idle fancies, very different from the reality. It is an uneasy sensation. Life becomes more complete when one is with the object of his attachment than ever before, but less complete at other times, for there is a constant sense of loss, as of something missing. Perhaps Adam felt that way when he awoke one morning and found one of his ribs missing. If so, he experienced the agreeable side of the sensation when he saw Eve beside him. When I was satisfied that my love for Nellie was reciprocated, I told her all—confessed my crime and pleaded my love in extenuation. She forgave all, and we were married a few weeks afterward. The first year of our married life was spent in European travel. Then we returned to Montreal, and Twok was born in that city. I wanted her to have a name that was all her own, and so I just put a few letters together at haphazard and formed the name Twok. When the child was a year old we went to Italy, where we remained for a year, when my wife died after a short illness. Then all my love centred in my child. I sailed for Canada with her. In my grief I kept aloof from the other passengers, only confiding to a sympathetic looking, grey-bearded old man the fact that my child was motherless, and that we had not a relation in the world. I said nothing about my wealth. In all those years when my loved ones were dying I had never once been sick myself, but now on shipboard I was stricken with typhoid fever. Twok was taken from me, as I afterward learned, by the old man whom I have mentioned, who was a basket maker by trade and was emigrating to Canada. He was very kind to my baby, but was terribly afraid of the fever, and did not come near me during my illness. So, when another man died of the disease and was buried at sea, it was not surprising that he got matters mixed, and, supposing that I was the dead man, went off with Twok. Well, I have been hunting for the old man and my child ever since, but, although I appealed to the police departments all over the continent, I was never able to find them. The old man must have died while she was very young. Now you have heard my story. Of course there is much to condemn, but a sort of retributive justice seems to have followed me through life. My mother died a few days after I stole Nelly; Nelly herself died just as I was learning what a beautiful thing the mother instinct is when developed in a lovely woman; and the child whom Nellie would have cared for so tenderly had she lived, disappeared while I was tossing helplessly in the delirium of fever. You will blame me, but perhaps you can pity me too."

The stranger pauses and looks at Joy wistfully. Joy says nothing, but offers his hand to Trenwith, who takes it and holds it for some time in silence. Then he says, "But where is she now? You have only told the story up to where she went to live with Dr. Somerville. I have already seen Dr. Somerville and he told me to come to you. Do not keep me longer in suspense. Surely she is not dead?"

"No. She has run away."

"Tell me all, young man," says Trenwith sternly. "Do not try to deceive me."

Joy tells the story of his love and its consequences, without mentioning Mary's name. The stranger hears him in silence, and then says coldly,

"She is little more than a child."

"You loved her mother when she was a child."

"Yes. I cannot blame you, and I know how much you have done for her through Dr. Somerville, from whom I heard most of the story. We must find her at once."

"She promised to write to Dr. Somerville, and he thinks it wisest to wait for her letter, as it may furnish a clue. If she thinks we are hunting for her she may take steps to elude pursuit."

"And am I to lose my child because you persecute her with undesired attentions?"

"I have never persecuted her. I have never said a word to her of love, and don't intend to do so. Had she remained a penniless orphan I might have done so, but I am well aware that a blacksmith is not a fit husband for an heiress."

"Then if you fulfil your engagement with the girl-to whom you are honorably bound at once, she will return without delay. I will pay you ten thousand dollars on your wedding day. It will be but a small return for the care you have taken of my child. Both she and I will even then owe you a debt of gratitude for life."

"You are very kind, but I do not want your money, nor can I marry anyone else. I can bear the thought of giving her up if she loves some one who is worthy of her, but I cannot banish her image from my mind and heart."

"Who is this young lady who has made so much trouble?"

"No young lady has made any trouble. The young lady is beautiful and good, and blameless in the matter, and while I have been both a fool and a coward, I am not quite mean enough to talk about her by name. I believe the only persons in Linklater who know about our engagement are her own mother and Dr. Somerville. Certain particulars I felt, under the circumstances of Twok's disappearance, bound to give you, but names are immaterial."

"You are right. I should not have asked. I beg your pardon. I suppose we will have to await developments, but I am very impatient. I have some business in Toronto tomorrow. If you learn anything further, telegraph to me, care of Swingly & Swornly, solicitors. In the meantime, good night."

Joy spoiled many sheets of note-paper that night trying to write a satisfactory letter of explanation to Mary, and did not stop writing until his supply of note-paper was exhausted. Then he went to bed to pass an uneasy night and awake unrefreshed in the morning. After a hurried breakfast he walked to the village postoffice to buy a fresh supply of paper.

"Here's a letter for you, Joy," said the postmaster.

Joy put it in his pocket and walked home without looking at it, but upon reaching the shop opened it eagerly. It was from Mary, and read as follows:

Dear Joy,
  You were never a very ardent lover. You wished once that you were my brother, and I think you have always acted like a brother—a very good brother. But a woman wants more than a brother's love, and cannot passionately love a man unless he first loves her in the same way. I think that is God's way of regulating things. Custom obliges the man to do the courting, and in order to protect the woman God prevents her from falling in love until she knows she is loved in the right way. At least that is my experience. I began to fancy some time ago that you did not love me as you ought to do, and was somewhat annoyed to find that the thought was not displeasing to me. You tried to make me give you up because you were poor and I was rich. I would not do that, but truly I wished that you were rich, too, in order that I might honorably break off the engagement. What you could not give me, someone else has, and, oh! my heart is longing to accept it. Will you give me a brother's blessing?
                Yours sincerely,   Mary Slemmings.

Joy did not waste any note-paper in writing the following answer:

Dear Mary,
  Love is like the wind which bloweth where it listeth and we can neither understand nor control it. I have watched you grow from a pretty child into a beautiful woman with a brother's pride. Now I hear of your happiness with a brother's pleasure. We are brother and sister again, as we always should have remained, and "someone else," whose name you have not told me, has secured a treasure.
              Yours very sincerely,   Joy Cougles.

CHAPTER IV.

THE firm of Swingly & Swornly was not very well known in Toronto, and its law practice was rather limited, but it had established something of a reputation as a private detective agency, although it never advertised itself as such, the partners preferring to be known to the public at large as barristers, solicitors and attorneys. They had more than once been of service to Trenwith in following up clues; not to a successful issue, it is true, but still in a way that pleased him. For the failure to find his daughter heretofore, neither the firm nor the detectives had been so much to blame as the clues. Now there was something substantial to work upon, and when he told them that after all his years of search he had found his daughter by chance and lost her again before he had an opportunity to claim her, they begged to be entrusted with the case and Trenwith willingly consented. It so happened that the only clerk in the employ of Swingly & Swornly was a law student, by name Samuel Slemmings, a very promising young man indeed, as Messrs. Swingly & Swornly explained to Trenwith. It was already understood that he was to become a partner in the firm so soon as he was admitted to the bar. Swingly, Swornly & Slemmings would sound alliterative and attract attention, besides Sam's father was wealthy, speculated in land, and it was worth while to have all his business transacted through them. It struck Messrs. Swingly & Swornly that the very person to hunt out the hiding place of a lovely young heiress, who had disappeared from Linklater, would be a clever young man who was born and brought up in Linklater, and this idea seemed so good that they communicated it to the young man himself, who informed them in turn, that he was acquainted with every nook and corner in and about Linklater, and that he and this young lady were friends, great friends in fact, and that he suspected she had run away to escape from the coarse attentions of a common blacksmith—not such a bad fellow in his way, if he would mind his own business, but still not one that a young lady of position like the runaway heiress in question could possibly fancy. True, this blacksmith had some knowledge of classics and mathematics; indeed he himself had taken lessons from him until he got beyond the capacity of his blacksmith teacher, but what was a smattering of Greek, Latin, Euclid and Algebra? Such studies might momentarily cover up the lowness of his nature and the rudeness of his training, but they could not change his character. That would show through it all whenever the real test came. Sam spoke with such emotion that the tears stood in his eyes, and he begged Swingly & Swornly to say nothing to the young lady's father about his intimacy with Miss Trenwith, for it was not for him to presume on a former acquaintance, when the girl was poor and friendless.

Sam learned that Trenwith had willed all his property, about one hundred thousand dollars, to Twok, making Dr. Somerville her guardian, in case he died before she came of age. He was not at all pleased to learn that Twok had a wealthy father and that she would inherit all his wealth. Not that he objected to a rich wife, but he thought if she were poor and he rich and honored, she could not reject his suit. Now she would have scores of wealthy suitors and his chances of success would be greatly lessened. So Sam, examining himself, found that he was not at all glad that Trenwith had turned up, and he was at first disposed to feel rather miserable. But he said to himself as he scrutinized himself, "This is proof that my love for Twok is real. If there had been anything sordid or mean in my love, I would be glad that she is rich, but I am sure I would rather that she were poor and friendless and nameless than that I should lose her."

Sam's examination of himself was very satisfactory to himself, and being a very promising young man, he wisely determined that it would not be at all in accord with the resolution and pluck he had hitherto displayed if he were to give up just because the girl whom he loved happened to be rich. This sensible conclusion being arrived at, it naturally followed that Sam, who had never been of a gloomy or desponding disposition, became very hopeful and thought it would be a very fine thing to have a rich wife. Of course he would not marry her for money; he would rather have Twok in poverty than the richest girl in America, but then since she was rich without any fault of his, why it would add very much to the attractiveness of married life, especially as he would be rich himself when his father died. These bright thoughts so occupied Sam that he never looked out of the car window until the train which carried him from Toronto to Hamilton passed over the Desjardins canal. Then he looked down the pretty bay while the train rattled along the Burlington Heights, and wondered whether he and Twok would ever have so fine a residence as Dundurn Castle. At Hamilton he took the stage for Linklater. The scenery was lovely, but Sam was too busy with his thoughts to notice it. Suppose she had left Linklater at once, all his trouble might be for nothing. Was there anyone in Linklater to whom Twok could flee? No. She had few acquaintances, and her only friends were Joy Cougles, Dr. Somerville, and perhaps the Linklaters. Why she had fled he could not imagine unless it were true as he told his employers, that she wished to escape from Joy's attentions. Trenwith had been silent in regard to this, and what other reason could there be? If he only knew why she had run away, there would be no great difficulty in finding her. Was there really any use looking for her in Linklater? Yes, he might find a clue there, even if he did not find her. Stay! she had some sort of an understanding with Carlock, the mysterious village crank. He had seen her going into his cabin years ago, and looking through the dirty panes of the little window, had seen the old man and the little girl disappear together in the cupboard, and then, after waiting for what seemed to him hours, had seen them come out again and had watched Twok go away. That had astonished him greatly, and he had concluded at the time that Carlock must have sold himself to the devil. Now, being so much older, and not believing in the existence of the devil, he tried to account in a rational way for the disappearance of the old man and the child in the cupboard, but without success. However, he thought it worth while to pay a visit to Carlock's house, and so before the stage reached the village he asked the driver to let him down, and taking the nearest path to the ravine, made his way toward the cabin. A rabbit crossing his path ran into a hole, and he threw a large stone after it. There was a rumbling sound, as if it had rolled some distance, and his curiosity being excited he cleared away the brush and stones, and soon made a wide opening.

"A cave!" he exclaimed in astonishment. "This may account for old Carlock's mysterious cupboard. He probably has a private entrance to this cave."

It was so dark inside that he could see nothing, but the cave seemed to him to be of considerable dimensions, and he determined to go home and return with a lantern to make explorations.

CHAPTER V.

IT is midnight, and the many trees on the hills of Linklater bend and sway and tremble as the wind whispers to the leaves that a great storm is coming. It is very dark except when the whole night seems bright with lightning, which shows the steep banks on either side of the ravine at Broadglance for a moment, and then leaves them in blacker darkness than before. Jasper Trenwith stands under the old elm where he found his wife and Twok's mother, caring nothing for the lightning and not at all disturbed by the pealing thunder. The same faculty which enables him to throw images upon the brain of a sleeper brings up those images with startling distinctness to himself, and as he stands there in the darkness, with the rain pelting against him and drenching him to the skin, his whole life passes before him like a panorama, and he looks at it with wretched anticipation, knowing always what is to follow, and feeling, even when the scene is one of supreme happiness, that it will be succeeded by one of misery. Now it is over. He has finished the past and is in the present. What will be the future? If he could see the future with the vividness that he can see the past. But what does it matter about him? If he could only know that Twok would be happy, he would be satisfied. She seems to be troubled with the same fatal rashness that has ruined his own life. Else why did she run away from friends whom she loved and who loved her? Jasper Trenwith is not a religious man, but he does not disbelieve in God; very few thinking men do. He has not prayed for years before, but now he does.

"O God! keep her from harm. Punish me, but bless her."

Hark! Is that an answer to his prayer? The night is gone. For a moment it is lighter than day. Every object stands out distinct and separate from the rest as it never does in daylight; but, clearest of all, the old elm and the tall handsome man who leans against it with clasped hands and upturned face. Then there is a crash of thunder that seems to shake the hills of Linklater, and wakes the sleeping villagers, in fear that their houses are falling about their ears, and Alvin going out early the next morning to see the wreck of the old elm tree, the top of which had been tossed over the embankment and into the deep pond in the ravine below, finds the form of Trenwith still leaning against the shattered trunk, with hands clasped and eyes reverently closed, as if he were still in prayer.

CHAPTER VI.

THE night seemed very long to Twok as she lay in her pretty bedchamber in the cave. She could not distinguish night from day in that place where sunlight never entered, but she knew when morning dawned, for a little Swiss clock on the wall counted off the hours. At six o'clock she dressed and prepared breakfast for herself over the gas stove, and having partaken of it took from the big blue box one of the knifemaker's yellow covered novels, and settled herself comfortably on a buffalo robe before the fire. It was not a good book to read—not at all a good book—not the sort of a novel that she had been accustomed to read, but just the sort of a book that would have brought a very deep blush to her face if Joy had found her reading it. And as she read it in that lonely underground room where no one could see her, it put thoughts into her head that made her blush even there and hide her face in her hands, as if someone were looking. And yet Twok read the book right through from cover to cover, after which she held it over the lighted gas until her fingers were quite badly burned, as if it were a satisfaction to her to see the pretty little nails blackened and scorched by the same flame that curled up the yellow covers. Then she threw the burning book on the clay floor and watched it resentfully as it turned black. After that she threw herself on the buffalo robe and sobbed as if her heart were broken, for a long time. Finally she knelt down on the bare floor and asked God to pardon her for her sinfulness, promising that she would never be so wicked again ; and I think if Joy could have witnessed the whole scene and understood her feelings, he would have taken the little girl in his arms very passionately, or else restraining himself, would have hammered the name of Twok out of all semblance of shape.

When Twok arose from her knees, she was so very tired that she lay down on her bed without undressing and slept very soundly for many hours. Whether it was day or night when she awoke she did not know, for the clock had stopped, but she was very hungry at any rate and proceeded to cook herself a piece of meat which she placed between two pieces of bread, and put the sandwich thus made between her pearly teeth in such an entrancing way, that she would have looked most provokingly charming if anyone had been there to see. All that day, or night, whichever it was, Twok waited patiently doing nothing. She might have amused herself reading novels, for there was still a whole boxful of books left, and some of them, no doubt, were very respectable, with nothing harmful in them. But Twok resolutely refused to look at one of them, and tried very hard to expel all ideas generated by the one she had read. At last she was startled by a sound of breaking glass, and looking up saw Sam Slemmings looking down at her from the window that shut Carlock's room off from the channel. She gazed at him in blank astonishment until he pushed himself through the broken window, and dropping to the floor said exultingly,

"So I have found you at last and will rescue you from the ogre. Where is the old monkey?"

At this moment footsteps were heard in the passage and Carlock opened the door.

"What are you doing here?" he said, glaring at Sam.

Sam drew a revolver from his pocket and presented it at the old man's head, but Twok sprang forward and standing directly in front of the knife maker, looked at Sam defiantly as she cried,

"Coward! Would you murder a defenceless old man?"

"I didn't intend to hurt him," said Sam, abashed.

"Then put down your revolver," she said.

He laid it on the table, saying, "Is this the thanks I get for all the trouble I have taken to rescue you from this chimpanzee?"

Carlock shook with rage for a moment, but recovering himself said,

"I have something to tell this young lady that is too sad to allow of my quarreling with you," and he looked at Twok with such compassion, and seemed to be so distressed, that she wondered if Joy could have killed himself in grief, and reproached herself for having left him, but when she found voice to say, "Oh, what has happened?" she was almost stunned by the answer, "Your father is dead. I think you should go to him."

"My father?" she faltered.

"Yes. It seems very strange, but from what I could learn of the story he lost you when you were a baby, and has been hunting for you ever since. Just when he found that you were in Linklater you ran away, and before he could discover your whereabouts he was struck dead by lightning. Of course you can't care much for him, never having seen him, but still it would look better to go and see him."

"Where is his—his body?"

"You will find him at Dr. Somerville's."

Without so much as a look at either Sam or Carlock, or a word of farewell, Twok stepped through the open door and walking along the passage ascended to the cabin and from it to the open air, climbed the path leading out of the ravine, and never stopped for breath until she reached the top of the hill and the road leading to the house of Dr. Somerville. She did not question the truthfulness of the old man's story, but walking quickly to the house entered without the formality of knocking and was met in the hall by the greatly astonished doctor.

"Where is my father?" she said, in a quiet, determined way, altogether different from the ordinary Twok. "I must see him."

Dr. Somerville said not a word, but slipping her arm through his led her into the room where Trenwith's coffined body lay. She gazed long and earnestly at his face in silence, but at last with a sob that told how much she felt, said,

"He was praying for me when he died. I know it."

"He was standing under the tree with his hands clasped and his eyes reverently closed when Alvin found him," said the doctor. "Certainly he was praying for some one, and why not for you, my poor Twok?"

"I am sure of it. I feel something saying so in my heart. Please tell me what you know."

The doctor told so much of Trenwith's story as he knew, which, indeed, was very little. When he told of Trenwith's grief on learning that she had run away just as he had found her, she broke down for the first time and sobbed most piteously. Still the doctor did not ask where she had been, but put his arm around her and would have led her from the room.

"Let me kiss him first," said Twok.

The warm red lips touched the cold pallid ones for a moment and then he led her unresistingly away to his library, where a bright fire was burning in the open grate, although the day was not cold. Seating her in an easy chair before the fire he took a small rocking chair himself and said,

"Now, my dear, tell me all about it. There was no need to run away. Joy is a good boy and will soon conquer this absurd passion and marry Mary."

Twok began to cry softly.

"There, there, you are not to blame," said the doctor.

"Oh, I am such a wicked girl," sobbed Twok.

"Well, well, don't cry. You didn't run away with Sam?"

"Oh, Dr. Somerville, how could you?" cried Twok, jumping up with such sudden anger that the doctor, in his astonishment, tipped his rocking chair too far back and fell sprawling on the floor. Then she helped him up so tenderly and asked so sweetly and so tearfully if he was very much hurt, that he felt quite remorseful and begged her forgiveness.

Twok told her story, carefully guarding the secret of Carlock's occupation, but telling Dr. Somerville that he should himself be able to sympathize with the lonely old man.

"And why, Twok?" he asked.

"Because he has a hobby as well as you, and such a queer one it is, but so horrible. You see he collects relics of murderers and murdered men. Why, I wonder I didn't see ghosts when he left me there alone, but I never once thought of that."

Both were silent for some time, but at last Twok said,

"What is my name?"

"Twok Trenwith."

"Then I will not have to change my first name?"

"No. That is the name your father gave you."

"I am glad of that, because it is the name that Joy hammered so," and Twok hid her blushing face in the cushions of her chair.

O blind doctor! did you see her do that? Did you notice the little ecstacy of pride with which she said that? No, you didn't, sir, and that is why you said in reply,

"Yes. It would be rather inconvenient to change the name now, but after all very few people will call you by your Christian name. You will be going away to get educated and will be known in future as Miss Trenwith, the heiress, so it wouldn't make much difference."

O stupid, dull-witted doctor! what were your eyes and ears made for? Do you really suppose that any pretty girl will ever give you her confidence after this?

CHAPTER VII.

JOY COUGLES of course met Twok at her father's funeral, but she acted in such a constrained way and treated him so coldly, that he went home afterward feeling very low spirited. His whole life seemed to him to have been a failure. There was Sam Slemmings, he thought, now rapidly developing into a successful lawyer. Dr. Somerville was right. If things went on in the same way for a few years longer Sam, who was once so much his inferior, would be his superior in every way. He had met Mr. Samuel Slemmings at the funeral, and that promising young man had bowed to him in a somewhat condescending way, and somehow Joy felt that Mr. Samuel Slemmings, student-at-law, could not be blamed for being a little condescending to a common blacksmith. But I am glad to say that in this gloomy state of mind, while he was contrasting himself and his prospects with Sam and his prospects, there was no feeling of hatred toward Sam. Even when he thought that Sam would be a more suitable husband for Twok than he would, there was only pity for himself. He did not blame himself in the least, however, but attributed it all to luck. "It is not my doing, or his doing, or God's doing," he said to himself. "It is only the undesigned result of many people acting and reacting on one another." But this thought did not make him the more hopeful. It would be just his luck, he thought, to go on in the same way all his life long. This was a most unpromising way for a young man to look at life; quite a different way from that in which Mr. Samuel Slemmings, student-at-law, was viewing it at the same time.

The said Mr. Samuel Slemmings was thinking to himself, "Some men have no ambition. They are careless and shiftless, and it is their own fault that they do not succeed. There is no such thing as luck in this world. Everyone could get along well enough if he looked after himself and his belongings as well as I do."

Mr Samuel Slemmings' way of looking at life was undoubtedly most promising, but I am not sure that he would have looked at it in that way if he had not had a rich father to give him some belongings to look after. And Joy's reflections gradually brought him around to an old idea to which the reflections of Mr. Samuel Slemmings never did lead. "After all," said Joy to himself, "I am better off than many others, and so long as I don't let my misfortunes hurt my character, they can't do me any permanent harm. And am I not hurting my character, spoiling my character, marring the man I am making by being so despondent?" This thought had a very good effect on Joy. It made him get up very energetically and set to work, whistling as he did so. The tunes he whistled were cheerful ones and sad thoughts would not chime in with them, so he had to change the thoughts to make them harmonize. And the thoughts that harmonized with the tunes he whistled were something after this pattern : " Perhaps I may be able to invent something out of which I can make a fortune. I will try at all events."

His work finished, he called on Alvin Linklater, who was about to leave the village to take a course in medicine at Toronto.

"And why don't you follow a profession, Joy?" said Alvin. "You know so much to begin with."

"I am afraid that I am too old to begin now."

"Why not become a minister?" You have a good voice and a clear head, and you have almost, if not quite, convinced me that there is a God, or perhaps more correctly that God is."

"I am not orthodox enough. No church would take me.

More than that, I am not sure enough that my own opinions are right to care to preach them."

"You are not beginning to doubt the existence of God?" said Alvin, in alarm.

"No. I will never do that. I do not see how any thinking man can. But whereas in the old days I differed from the orthodox and made new doctrines to suit myself and still accord with the Bible, feeling perfectly sure that I was right, now I cannot dogmatize on these points. I am now an agnostic; I was a bigot before. But this much I believe, there is a great God who fills the universe, and that He is working out some great, grand purpose, to which all things tend. I believe, too, that God is Law as God is Love, and that holding His purpose in view He cannot alter many things as He would otherwise do. Knowing that men will become grander and nobler if they are allowed to work out their own destinies, He is obliged to allow them to act and react on one another, and so causes His sun to shine alike on the just and the unjust."

"You call yourself an agnostic. Are not the terms infidel and agnostic synonymous?"

"No. They are often interchanged, but it is a misusage of terms. An infidel is as dogmatic and bigoted as a Roman Catholic, only in a different way. The great difference is that the infidel's dogmatism is egotistical. The Roman Catholic says there is a God, because the fathers of his church have told him so; the infidel says there is no God, because he cannot see him. One is as positive as the other. Neither will admit the possibility of his being in the wrong. The agnostic simply says, 'I don't know.' Now I am not an agnostic in the strict sense of the word. I do most emphatically believe in God. I am as sure of that as I am of my own existence. Everything in nature proves it. I know that in Him we live and move and have our being. But I am not so sure about the inspiration of the Bible. I have strong doubts about that, and I am not sure that I understand who Jesus was. Of this much I am sure, that he was good and wise and loving, and that to make ourselves like him is the highest aim that any of us can have. If God allows us to make ourselves, He has not left us without a model."

"Preach that, Joy. It will do good."

"No. There are churches enough already without starting another. Everything that is essential is already taught by the churches, and if they mix up with their teaching many things that are not essential I can't help that. Besides, if I were a preacher I might sometimes advance opinions that I would afterwards be sorry for. So long as thought remains unexpressed it is under our control; it is, as it were, a part of ourselves. But let the thought be communicated to others, either in speaking or in writing, and it enters upon a life of its own. It becomes an existence as separate from ourselves as the child from its mother. We can no longer control it; it may to a certain extent control us. It presents itself in different lights to different minds, and exerts a varied influence upon them, always calling into life new thoughts and often changing the force of old ones. It becomes, in short, a living, active thing which may exert a mighty influence on the world."

"Is thought a creation, then?"

"I do not think so. The same thought often originates in the brains of different men. I sometimes think that thought is a grasping after the eternal, unchanging truth. The truth is always there, but we can seldom get at it. We can never see it clearly; we look through a glass darkly. And yet sometimes we get a glimpse of it as we look through the darkened glass of the brain, and some men having clearer glasses than others get a better view. And that, I think sometimes, is the way the Bible was inspired. They were clear brained men, those old prophets of the Bible. Inheriting strong, healthy bodies from their parents, they kept them pure and undefiled by living rightly, and their simple life out under God's sky was very favorable to contemplation. It kept the glasses of their brains so clear and unobscured that they sometimes saw through them right into the mind of God. And yet even their glasses were sometimes obscured. A little speck on the glass, or a little unevenness in it, would distort the truth. Then having looked at the truth clearly, or caught a glimpse of it darkly, they had to paint a word picture to show it to others, and those word pictures, in the form of the Bible, have come down to us through the ages. Is a picture ever exactly true to nature? I think not. Neither do words ever exactly describe thoughts."

"That is a new idea of the Bible."

"I don't know that it is new. So many things that I have thought out I have afterward found to be old ideas, that I am very cautious now. It is original with me. I have never heard of anyone who looked at it just in that way, but the same idea has probably occurred to other men."

"I think I understand you, and I believe that your glass is clearer than that of most men. Anyhow, it must be gratifying to look at the truth through your own glass, even if it does get a little dirty sometimes and obscure things, instead of only looking at the pictures painted by others. I suppose a bigot is a man who thinks that his glass is always clear."

"That is the idea exactly. A bigot may be a very clear headed man, or he may see through his glass darkly. He is a bigot in either case if he thinks he always sees clearly and cannot be persuaded that there may possibly be specks on his glass that obscure the truth a little. The bigot doesn't necessarily see through his own glass at all. He very commonly looks only at the pictures painted by others, the fathers of his church, and his bigotry then consists in supposing that those pictures are without any possibility of doubt exactly true to nature."

"It was very strange," said Alvin as they were parting at the gate, "That my dream was so nearly exact, was it not?

Twok's father some time ago wrote the story of his life and put it in a sealed envelope, which he left with Swingly & Swornly, of Toronto, instructing them to forward it to my father in case of his death. My father received it and gave it to me to read. It corresponds exactly with my dream."

Joy told him how Trenwith had stood over him that night as he slept under the tree. In conclusion he said,

"You talked of falling in love with Twok. You would not wish to marry your cousin?"

"No, I don't believe in cousins marrying. Of course she is only half a cousin. Her mother was my father's half sister. But even if we were not related, I am not so foolish as to think she would fall in love with a homely, awkward fellow like me. I am not ugly, but I am very far from handsome. Looks don't count for much in making friendships, but they are everything in love making. But I am not in love with Twok. If I were, I could not bear the thought of her marrying anyone else, and really if she selects a man who is worthy of her, I believe I will take the same pleasure in seeing her married that I would in the fitting conclusion of a novel. I will be an old bachelor. I have an idea that if I ever fall in love it will be with someone so much better than myself that there will be no hope for me. You see I have an exceedingly good taste. I think I will try to be a politician. A fellow must have something to be enthusiastic about. If he can't love a woman, the next best thing is to love his country, and I do love Canada. Moreover, I have always taken a great interest in politics."

As Alvin walked up to the house he said to himself, "Joy would make a fine husband for Twok if he only had a profession. I must try to persuade him to be a doctor."

[END OF PART II.]

PART III.

CHAPTER I.

MISS Charlotte Somerville was one of those charming old maids of whom people say, "I wonder why no one ever fell in love with her." At the age of forty she had still a lovely face, a clear complexion, a graceful figure, and a fascinating manner. She had a well trained voice, not very strong, but very sweet, and was an accomplished pianist. She had read the best books, could talk entertainingly about them, and might have written very interesting books herself had she been so disposed. Many people imagine that all a man has to do to secure a girl in marriage is to fall in love with her, and then tell her about it. But girls do not always happen to fall in love with the men who love them. The fact that a woman is single at forty does not necessarily indicate that she has been less attractive than her married sisters. There are many unlovable old maids, just as there are many disagreeable married women, but as a class they have been cruelly slandered. The loveliest and sweetest girls, the ones who are most sought after, sometimes become old maids. Miss Somerville had had many opportunities to marry, but the one whom she would have accepted had never offered himself, and she would not marry anyone else. It was a sore disappointment to her, but no one ever knew her secret sorrow. She was not nearly so happy as she would have been as the wife of the man she loved and the mother of his children. Whether she was happier cherishing that love than she would have been as the wife of another man, I cannot say, but at all events, having a many-sided character, she took a great deal of enjoyment out of life. She was never so happy as when making other people happy. Many a poor family had reason to bless her, and the little social gatherings at her house had often been the means of introducing to each other, young people, who were so well pleased with one another that they chose to walk through life together. Some people said that Miss Somerville was a match-maker—a dreadful charge to make against an old maid ; but she always declared that it could not possibly be true, because marriages were made in heaven. She was not wealthy, but had been left a competence by her father, and had a very prettily furnished house in the West End of Montreal. The most charming people sometimes make mistakes, and Miss Somerville one day invested her little fortune in a speculation which promised to be very profitable, but which was so complete a failure that she found herself with nothing left but her house and furniture. Charlotte Somerville was not a woman to be discouraged by loss of fortune. Instead of lamenting over her losses, she said to herself cheerfully, "Well, it will teach me a lesson, and it might have been worse. The house and furniture might have gone, too. I am not the first woman who has had to work for her living. I will give music lessons."

Before she had an opportunity to ask the patronage of her friends in her new undertaking she received from her cousin, Dr. Somerville, of Linklater, the following letter, which somewhat altered her plans :

LINKLATER, December 16.

MY DEAR CHARLIE,

As if it were not enough to have Twok Trenwith to look after, my friend, Miss Jennie Hammond, dying, has left ten thousand dollars to her niece, Jennie Stone, on condition that half of it is spent under my direction in securing a fashionable education, and I have to see that the provisions of the will are carried out. The girl's merit consists in being called Jennie Hammond Stone. Why that should entitle her to a bequest, is more than I can say. I have called on the young lady. She is a rather handsome girl, tall and well formed, with red hair and freckles,

but very regular features, and lovely brown eyes. She talks very sensibly and is very well educated, having attended the High School at the village a few miles from her home for several years and passed the intermediate examination, which is the same as the literary examination for second class teachers' certificates. But she has no accomplishments. She can't play on the piano or sing or dance or speak French, and knows nothing of society. Then there is my adopted daughter, Twok. My wife and I have been travelling with her for some months, visiting all the leading cities of America, and now I wish to send her to some place where she can finish her education. You know what she is like. Could you not take the two girls and make fashionable ladies out of them ? Money is no object. You need not teach them yourself unless you wish. Engage masters for them in any subjects you do not care to undertake yourself. All you will have to do is to supervise their studies and show them something of society. I heard of your unfortunate speculation with great regret, but it is an ill wind that blows nobody good, and if it will dispose you to undertake the education of my wards they and I will have reason to be everlastingly thankful. Please let me hear from you soon.'
Your affectionate cousin,
ALEX. SOMERVILLE.

What resulted from this letter may best be shown by the budget of letters with which this chapter closes :

MONTREAL, January 25.
MY DEAR HALF-BROTHER,

Now that seems a rather funny way to open a letter, my first letter to you, but if it sounds cold it isn't intended to be so, for I am sure I love you just as well as if you were a whole brother. I arrived here in safety after a tiresome journey on the train, as you have probably heard already from mother, to whom I wrote sometime ago. A lot of foreign looking men, dressed in furs, were standing outside the station beside their one-horse sleighs, chattering French to one another, but when I looked around in dismay, wishing that the time I wasted in studying Latin at the High School had been occupied in learning to speak French, one of the chatterers stepped forward and asked me in very good English if I wanted a sleigh. Feeling much relieved, I gave him the checks for my trunks, and telling him Miss Somerville's address, was soon driving furiously along a rather narrow street, lined with very handsome stone buildings. Well, I won't describe the journey to the house. It didn't take long to get there, although it is a long way from the station, for the hackmen or carters, as they call them here, drive much faster than in Hamilton or Toronto. I felt rather nervous, expecting to be met by a somewhat stern looking old maid, who would probably kiss me on the cheek or forehead and bid me welcome in frigid tones, or else one who would gush over me as if I were her dearest friend, but the sweetest little woman came out of the house to meet me, and I could hardly be persuaded that it was Miss Somerville. She did not offer to kiss me at all, but took my hand so warmly and beamed on me so kindly out of her bright eyes that, I felt at home at once. I have since learned that she does not approve of promiscuous kissing among women. She thinks kissing should be reserved for those we love dearly, whether they be men or women, and as I received from her last night a sweet good-night kiss after I had been here three weeks, I feel almost like worshiping her. But I foresee that this is going to be a dreadfully long letter, and will therefore say nothing more about Miss Somerville until I have told you about someone who is even lovelier than she is. I mean the other pupil. Do you remember that many years ago when you and I were keeping house together while the folks were away, you brought home with you a very queer looking man and a very pretty little girl, who called themselves Jake and Twok Jakwok. I was an ignorant tomboy at that time, but it made a great impression on my mind. Still I would never have recognized the little girl in the fashionable heiress, Miss Trenwith, if she had not recognized me. She has the strangest story. Her mother died in Italy when she was a baby. Her father was bringing her to Canada on a ship when he was taken ill, and an old basket maker ran away with her, supposing him dead. He was very kind so long as he lived, but he soon died in Buffalo, leaving her in charge of a wicked old woman, from whom she ran away with this Jake who came to us. He left her with a learned blacksmith, a sort of demi-god, I should judge, from Twok's description of him. He and his mother adopted her and educated her until the mother died, when she went to live with Dr. Somerville, *my* Dr. Somerville. Her father found her at last, but was killed by lightning before she saw him. After her father's death, the doctor, who was appointed guardian, arranged with someone else to take his practice, and spent four months travelling all over the United States and Canada with his wife and Twok. Then he sent her to Miss Somerville to complete her education. She is very wealthy and has every wish gratified. Do you remember what the little girl looked like, and does the enclosed photograph remind you at all of her? You will agree with me that it is a rather pretty face. You have seen prettier ones probably. I certainly have. But the photograph does not do her justice. I don't think it would be possible to photograph her as she looks. There are several names by which various sorts of female comeliness may be described. They are handsome, pretty, beautiful and lovely. Now please don't call me vain when I say my looking-glass assures me that I am becoming a handsome woman, but I am neither pretty nor beautiful, and I am very far from lovely. A beautiful woman is both pretty and handsome. A lovely woman is both pretty and good. Pretty girls are often selfish and disagreeable, but lovely girls are always sweet and loving and unselfish.

Prettiness is purely material; loveliness is *spirituelle*. Mere prettiness is apt to last only for a few years; loveliness endures forever. Now Twok Trenwith's features are not remarkably pretty. They are rather pretty, and that is all that can be said for them. But she is the loveliest girl I ever saw. Let me describe her: She has a wealth of hair as soft as silk, reaching far below the waist. Its color—well I hardly know what to call it, unless it is sunny. It is darker than when you saw her and would probably be called brown in the shade, but when the sun is shining on it, it is a shimmer of gold. Then her complexion is almost perfect. She tells me she has been out in the sunshine a great deal and she seems to like it still, but it has not spoiled her complexion in the least, but seems rather to have given it a peculiarly charming tint. But the strangest thing about her face is the expression. She has so many expressions. I believe anyone very well acquainted with her could read her thoughts and feelings by them. In looking at her, you feel almost as if you were looking through her face at her soul. You can't photograph a soul, and that is why her portrait isn't like. No doubt the features are like in the photo, but the expressions are not there. I think when she dies her dead face will look more like her photograph than like herself, and if she has a friend who does not believe in a future life, he will change his mind when he sees it. He cannot fail to be impressed with the fact that it was a lovely indwelling spirit that made her features so expressive. But this letter is already altogether too long, so I must close for this time with love to your wife and baby.

Your affectionate sister,

JENNIE STONE.

P. S.—Please send back the photo at once.

J. H. S.

MONTREAL, February 2.

DEAR JOY,

I have waited and waited for you to write to me, and now I am going to write first. Perhaps you will say that as I was travelling about and you were all the time in one place, I should have written to you. But how was I to know that you were attending medical lectures in Toronto, when you sold your shop and went away from Linklater without sending me any word? I knew you had gone; that was all. If I seemed cold and unnatural to you at the time of my father's funeral, it was partly because I was so bewildered with the strangeness of it all and partly because I was ashamed of having run away. Please to forgive me, Joy, and write to me sometimes, for I became so accustomed to having a brother during the years I lived with you and your mother that I feel entirely lost without one. You have heard from Dr. Somerville that I am living with his cousin, Miss Charlotte Somerville. He has told you all the particulars, but I must say in addition that I love her very much already. I don't think anyone could help loving her, she is so gentle and good and refined. You have heard, too, I suppose, that there is another pupil besides myself, a Miss Jennie Stone, but you probably do not know that it is the same Jennie Stone who gave me bread and milk in a farm-house when I was tramping with Jake many years ago. Poor Jake! I wonder where he is now. I have advertised for him, and Dr. Somerville has written to the police of a great many cities, but all to no purpose. Always when we were travelling I was looking out for him, but never saw him. Then there is old Meg. We tried to find her, too. Perhaps she is dead. I feel very sorry for her now. She may never have had anyone to teach her to be good. I might have been still worse myself, but for you and your dear mother. But I started to tell you about Jennie Stone. She is a handsome girl, very clever, and good, too. She has red hair and freckles, but I think they are very becoming to her. It is a nice shade of red, and the freckles are really rather pretty. She and I agree very well together, except about the Roman Catholics. There are so many of them here, and I think it is best to be friendly with them, but she, who is full of kindness for everybody else, is so bitter against the priests, that I fear she would burn them at the stake, if she had the opportunity. One day we were crossing a square in front of Notre Dame church, when she stumbled and fell. There had just been a thaw, and the snow was quite muddy, so that her sealskin jacket was covered with dirt. I tried to rub it off with my handkerchief, but she said,

"Wait a minute. I know what to do."

Then she walked right into the church and, dipping her handkerchief into the holy water fount, deliberately sponged off her jacket with it. I was quite horrified, although I did not in the least regard the water as sacred, for it seemed wrong to violate what others held sacred, and then if the priests had seen her, there might have been serious trouble. Fortunately no one noticed what she was doing. Now I don't think that was a sensible thing to do, but I could not help admiring her for it. One always feels that she is true. She believes in what she says and does, and would not sacrifice a principle for anything. That is noble, and I love her for it.

Now I think I have written quite enough to merit a reply, and I hope you will tell me all about yourself and what you are doing.

Yours sincerely,

TWOK TRENWITH.

TORONTO, February 4.

MY DEAR TWOK,

Forgive me for my long silence. It was certainly not due to forgetfulness of you. After you had gone, there seemed to be an emptiness about Linklater, and I could not stay there. At first I thought of trying for a situation in some large machine shop in one of the big American cities, but finally decided to become a professional man. I am rather old to begin, but when one considers that the years of man's life are three score and ten, what do four or five years amount to? I will not have quite enough money to take me through, although I obtained a good price for my property in Linklater; but the holidays are long, and I can easily earn enough at my trade to put me through when my bank account is exhausted.

The shop was sold to old Mr. Well, who used to have a blacksmith shop in the next concession, and I thought he intended to run it himself, but he gave it to his nephew, Dick, who worked in his shop years ago, but afterward ran away to the States, engaged in various light-fingered employments, I am told, and finally served a term in penitentiary. His uncle thinks he has reformed now, but I can assure you that I don't at all like the idea of having him in charge of the old place.

You have heard, I suppose, of Mary's marriage to a Chicago gentleman, an old Hamilton man, who met her while home on a visit. Their courtship seems to have been short and decisive. He was well off and wanted a wife at once, and there was no necessity for delay after the preliminaries were arranged.

I am very glad that you are so pleasantly situated, and am quite anxious to see Miss Somerville, of whom both you and Dr. Somerville think so highly, and Miss Stone, who seems to be a young lady of considerable character.

I meet Sam Slemmings on the street occasionally. He seems to be cutting quite a swell here. The other day he stopped and condescendingly offered to recommend me to any of his friends who wanted repairing done, although he knew I was studying medicine. I am afraid that I am developing into a snob, for I felt quite insulted at the proposal, although that is the kind of work I can do best. However, I restrained my foolish indignation, and told him that I was too busy to oblige his friends in that way and that he had better look up someone else. He then said he was going to Montreal in a few days, and asked if I had any message to send to Twok, to which I replied that I had no message to send to Miss Trenwith. Without any of the old hate in my heart, I must say that from what I can hear, he is not improving in character.

You may be sure, Twok, that I will answer promptly any letters you may send me, and I will count the days between them.

Yours sincerely,

JOY COUGLES.

TORONTO, January 28.

MY DEAR DR. SOMERVILLE,

Please keep a watch on Sam Slemmings. I do not know exactly what importance to attach to what he says, but he talks as if he were on very familiar terms with Twok, and I know he has met her several times since I have. I am afraid he is making love to her. You may ask, what business that is of mine and say he has as much right to love her as I have. Well, I am not making love to her just now, and I think, after the care I took in teaching her, that I have a right to look after her in a brotherly way. If she marries someone who is worthy of her, all right; but I cannot bear the thought that she who is so pure and good should marry him. He is getting along very well in the study of law, I understand, and will probably be a successful lawyer, but he is living what is called a fast life, only sowing his wild oats, people say; but I know and you know that three-fourths of the men who sow wild oats in their youth go on doing so all their lives. The only difference is that they are rather proud of it as boys, while as married men and church members, they are forced to dissipate on the quiet. Sam is handsome, has lots of money, and has been for several years taking lessons in dancing, music and like accomplishments. He can sing a good song, and makes a very agreeable addition to any party, so that he has obtained admission to very good society here in spite of his father's old occupation, which is a drawback to him. There is, undoubtedly, very much to admire in him, and in the eyes of most people he is a very good fellow, but it is not mere jealousy that makes me say that he is too much of an animal to be the husband of pure little Twok. You are her guardian. For pity's sake, ask Miss Somerville to warn her in some way.

Yours truly,

JOY COUGLES.

TORONTO, January 28.

MY DEAR ALVIN,

I am very glad to hear that you have quite recovered from your illness. When I called on you on the day of Mr. Trenwith's funeral and talked to you about becoming a professional man, we little thought that I would begin the study of medicine before you. I am sorry that you have decided to study in Montreal instead of Toronto, because I would like you to be with me, but you may be right in saying that the hospital facilities are better there.

If you will not be offended at a little advice from an old friend, let me say this: You will meet with more temptations than you imagine among a lot of students in a big city. Do not be persuaded into any kind of evil-doing because " every fellow does it." You cannot remember your mother as I can mine, or I would say: Never do anything that you would be ashamed to talk to your mother about. Perhaps you can think of her as watching over you. Anyhow, you can remember that God is looking at you and thinking about you all the time. Be pure in action, thought and conversation. Anything that cannot stand the glare of the sunlight and the eyes of the purest men and women, is not fit to meet the eye of God. Remember that you are making yourself. It is an awful responsibility. Be careful not to spoil the work. Copy the model.

Yours truly,

JOY COUGLES.

CHAPTER II.

IT was perhaps unfortunate for Sam Slemmings that Joy Cougles letter reached Twok about an hour before he called on her. Still he was politely although coldly received. Twok was tastefully dressed and looked very stylish. He was greatly impressed, but did not feel at all ill at ease, for he was also stylishly dressed, and his face was covered with a brown beard that hid the scar and made him look quite handsome. Moreover, he was a most promising young man, and no one knew it better than he did. To be sure his father had been a butcher at one time, but then he had given up that business now and was confining his attention to real estate transactions—a very respectable business. Mary was well married, and the other children would receive a good education and have a fair start in life, so that his family relations would not disgrace him. Twok's father was dead. Dr. Somerville, who was her guardian, had always been very friendly with his father, and for the matter of that he himself had always been on good terms with the doctor, who certainly would not very strongly oppose an energetic young man with such brilliant prospects. Such were the thoughts that passed through his brain as he sat there talking to Twok.

"And how do you like Montreal, Twok?" he said.

"Very much, Mr. Slemmings; but Miss Trenwith, if you please."

"Oh, I beg your pardon, Miss Trenwith; but you called me Sam once, and gave me permission to call you Twok."

"I was only a little girl then. Now I am a young woman."

"But you don't seem to be a bit bigger now than then."

"I cannot help my littleness."

"You are not too small ; you are just right according to my taste. Your very littleness and your pretty little ways charm me almost as much as your beauty, so that I can scarcely refrain from taking you in my arms."

" Mr. Slemmings, you are rude and ungentlemanly."

" But how can I help telling you that I love you and that I have for years."

" I cannot listen to such talk as this."

"You encouraged me before."

" I had done you an injury, and wished to be kind to you as a sort of reparation, for it made me feel very sorry to think I had scarred your face. But now it is all covered up with a handsome beard, and as that scar will prevent your shaving, I don't know but what I have done you a service in preserving such a pretty beard."

" Now you are making fun of me."

" No, not at all. I mean all I say."

" I will shave it all off and let the scar show again if it will make you like me any better," and Sam stroked his beard regretfully.

" How absurd ! If you like to spoil your looks, you may do so. It will not be my fault. You need not have a scar show now unless you wish. And really, Mr. Slemmings, you very richly deserved the scar for your rudeness."

" I do not deny it, Miss Trenwith, but you must make allowances for a boy, and really you were most provokingly pretty even then. I don't want to seem vain, but I do think I have improved myself a good deal since then. With your help, I can make a noble man of myself. Don't drive me to the devil."

"Oh, I am sure you have improved, and I do hope you are trying to be good ; but you must be good for yourself, for the sake of being good and doing right, not on my account. I am afraid a man who would go to the devil because a woman refused him would carry her to the devil with him if she accepted."

"I do not despair of having you yet. I am not easily thwarted in a purpose I form. I will be rich and successful in a few years, and your fortune will not stand in my way then But how is our blacksmith friend getting along? I met him on the street and offered him some work the other day, but he did not seem to take it kindly."

"A blacksmith is just as good as a lawyer."

"I made no distinction between them. Blacksmithing undoubtedly is a very honest trade. It was you who made the distinction. I called him a blacksmith, but I have no objection to being called a lawyer."

"It was not what you said, but how you said. Your tone was insulting. But, Mr. Slemmings, has not this interview lasted long enough? Can either of us gain anything by prolonging it?"

So Mr. Samuel Slemmings made his bow, and went away not feeling nearly so much discouraged as a less promising young man might have felt under the circumstances. After his return to Toronto he wrote to her, setting forth his love and his prospects, saying he was determined to persist in spite of her refusal, and asking her to at least correspond. She answered this letter at once with a short note stating that it was useless to persist, nothing could change her mind, and she would not answer any more letters. To this he replied, reproaching her for having encouraged him, insinuating that she rejected his advances because of his father's former business, and concluding with the statement that he intended to renew his suit at a later date. This note was burned unanswered.

CHAPTER III.

TWOK replied to Joy's letter, and they kept up a regular correspondence after that. Joy never waited more than three days before answering a letter, but Twok sometimes waited for several weeks. When the intervals between the letters were longer than usual he would grow anxious and wonder if he had offended her in any way in his last letter. Sometimes while listening to lectures, at college, he would become strongly impressed with the idea that a letter was waiting for him at his boarding-house. This feeling did not prevent him attending diligently to the lectures, but as soon as they were over he would walk home with a sort of feverish haste, usually to be disappointed. When the letter did come he always carried it in his pocket for a few days, and read it over many times before putting it away with the rest, and often he would jump up suddenly while working at his medical books in his room at night, saying to himself, " I must have another look at the dear little girl's letters." Sometimes he would read all the letters through in order of date, comparing one with another; sometimes he would select one from the pack. He must have wasted a great deal of time in this way, but it did not prevent him passing a very creditable examination in the spring. Twok also carried on a friendly correspondence with Alvin Linklater, but letters only passed between them about once in six weeks, neither being very impatient to reply, although the correspondence was mutually agreeable and afforded a great deal of enjoyment to both. Joy often wished that he could contemplate the idea of Twok's marriage with someone else with the calm satisfaction that Alvin Linklater did. To him the thought of seeing her married to anyone, be he never so worthy, was most painful. He had always before had a sort of contempt for mere love stories, but now he developed an extraordinary liking for them. He knew how to sympathize with the lovers as he never did before, and then Twok always enacted the part of the heroine. One thing puzzled him. While Twok was seldom absent from his waking mind, he hardly ever dreamed about her. Joy never made mention of love in his letters. Alvin sometimes did, but it was in an abstract way, without any personal application, and Twok never imagined that he would ever ask to be more than a friend.

Twok and Jennie Stone studied together and grew to be very fond of one another and of their instructress. Miss Somerville had a large number of callers, both young and old, and the two girls made a great many acquaintances. The girls were sitting together one afternoon, taking turns in reading aloud George Macdonald's novel, "Sir Gibbie," when Alvin Linklater was announced. Twok received him most cordially and introduced him to Jennie as her cousin.

"How did you leave all our friends at Linklater?" she asked when they were seated.

"They are all very well."

"You have been ill yourself. I hope you have quite recovered."

"Yes. I am quite well again, but my illness has kept me back a year in my studies. Miss Stone was reading aloud when I came in?"

"Yes," said Jennie. "We have been taking turns about in reading aloud. It is 'Sir Gibbie,' a charming book. Have you ever read it?"

"One of George Macdonald's novels. Yes. I like all his books, but I think he makes more of his men than of his women in nearly all of them. He always brings in a noble man, great in body and mind and soul. The women are kept more in the background. You don't get so well acquainted with them, so to speak."

"Perhaps," said Twok, "it is because he can judge of men's thoughts and feelings by experience, but can only guess at those of women."

"How far have you read? I don't wish to spoil the story for you by disclosing the plot in any way," said Alvin.

"Oh, you needn't be afraid of that," said Jennie. "We have both read it before, but thought it would be nice to read it again together."

"Yes," said Twok. "You see we like to talk about the characters. You can't discuss the characters of people whom you meet in real life for fear of hurting somebody's feelings; but you can criticize the characters in a book to your heart's content, and so acquire a better insight into human nature."

"George Macdonald is not at all orthodox in his religious views," said Alvin.

"No," said Jennie. "He is a Universalist, and I am almost persuaded to be one, too. I cannot think of God as a vengeful being who would cause any one to suffer eternally. A loving father will punish his children to make them better, but can you imagine a father with a particle of love in his heart consigning his child to everlasting torments, knowing that the punishment will not make him better."

"No," said Twok, "but perhaps he can't help it. I think it is impossible for God to do some things, although we regard Him as omnipotent. For instance, God cannot make two equal to four. In other words He cannot make a part equal to its whole. That is self evident, but there may be moral laws which we do not fully understand that are just as unalterable as the relations of the numbers."

"That would mean that law is greater than God," said Alvin.

"No, not necessarily. Joy says God is Law, that Law is only a mode of action of the divine will."

"What does Joy say about future punishment? You and I are both disciples of Joy, but you have had more of his teaching than I have."

"Yes," said Twok, blushing. "Joy says if God makes hell, it is only a purgatory. If hell is eternal it is of man's own making, the misery naturally resulting from continuance in sin, but he is inclined to think that wicked people die of their sins. He says Jesus so often talked of eternal life and mourned because the people would not come to him to learn how they might secure it, that there must be such a thing as eternal death. He did not mean life in the body, but spiritual life, and the opposite of spiritual life is spiritual death. Now what happens when the body dies? It is gradually resolved into its original elements, the various gases of which it is composed. So with spiritual death. When a man's spirit dies it is simply resolved into its original elements and absorbed into the divine essence. He loses all individuality. Joy puts it in this way: God tries to persuade men to be good, to be at one with Him. He cannot force them without destroying their free will, and consequently annihilating their spiritual nature. This power to annihilate He constantly exercises, or else the universe would soon be so full of evil that there would be no room for the good. Violation of law always brings its own punishment. Violation of the laws of health causes disease of the body and finally induces death. Violation of spiritual laws makes the soul diseased, and, persisted in, brings about spiritual death."

"Do you believe that?" demanded Jennie.

"Well, I don't know. I am just telling you what Joy said, but I think it is a beautiful law that makes evil self destroying, that makes evil things die out while the good and pure and lovely endure forever. It is certain that that is the law of material things. Just so soon as anything in nature begins to lose its purity and beauty, it begins to decay and die. Is it not probable that the same law holds good in spiritual things? A great many people think that they can go on indulging sinful desires because God will make allowance for their weaknesses and make them good at last. If all men would understand that every indulgence in sin makes the soul diseased, and that a diseased soul is even harder to cure than a diseased body, the world would be better and purer than it is."

"That idea that a bad man is resolved into the divine essence is pure Buddhism," said Alvin.

"No, Jennie and I were reading about Buddhism the other day, and it struck me that the great distinction between Buddha and Christ was that while the former thought the great end to be aimed at was escape from individuality, and absorption in the divine essence, the latter thought the great end was to escape absorption or death and to preserve that individuality in accord with God, at one with God, but separate from Him. Their ethics were almost precisely the same, but their conception of the future was entirely different."

"That gives me a new idea," said Alvin. "I think I now understand something that often puzzled me before. I could never see why Christ suffered such agony in anticipation of death on the cross. In the early days of the Christian church many men suffered death in the same way for conscience sake. It was undoubtedly a terrible death, but I have never heard of any one else dreading it so much as to sweat great drops of blood. Now Joy says Christ came to the world to reveal to mankind the character of God, to show how God would live and act if he were a man, and so furnish us with a model. Suppose that after his work was accomplished he had to give up his individuality and become again a part of the divine essence. That would explain the meaning of the verse, 'He came forth from God and goeth unto God.' He no doubt fully understood all the great possibilities of an individual existence. The thought that he must himself give up that eternal life which he had taught others to value, would be agonizing."

"Oh, I hope not," said Twok. "It has been such a comfort to me when I felt lonely and forsaken, to feel that he might care for me, and that when I die I could go and talk to him. We may need him to teach us in heaven as much as we do here."

"Besides," said Jennie, "he appeared to his disciples after his death, which he could not have done if your supposition were correct."

"There is something in that," said Alvin. "Still his spiritual death might have occurred after he took his final farewell of the world."

"How about Saul's vision when he was struck blind?" said Twok.

"Well, Saul may have had a vivid imagination."

"Oh," said Twok, "if you want to account for things you do not understand in that way, why not suppose the disciples exaggerated the agony of Christ? It is much easier to believe that, than to suppose that the learned Saul and all his company were so badly deceived. Your supposition is not at all in accordance with Joy's theory. If what is good and pure endures forever, how could Jesus, who was perfectly good, ever die? Joy seems to think of Christ as an embodiment of the humanity of God. He does not believe that Jesus was God, but thinks he brought God within human ken, showing the likeness between God and man. But the world has seen so little of Jesus, although we have heard much about him, and Christianity is so far from universal, that his life would seem only a partial success if it ended here; but if we suppose that his earthly life was merely a prelude to the life eternal, and that when we enter the spirit world he will be to us always the divine interpreter, he seems a grand success. I have sometimes thought that Jesus is the eye of God."

"The eye of God!" exclaimed Jennie.

"Yes. If you look at a man's eyes in the right way, you can tell what his soul is like almost as well as if you met him in heaven. The eyes express shades of thought and feeling that words cannot convey. The eyes can picture love as nothing else can. Yet the eye is not the soul, nor is it the only medium through which we can catch glimpses of the soul. So Christ is not God, but through him we can see God most clearly."

Miss Somerville had entered the room unobserved, while Twok was speaking. Now she came forward, and, Alvin having been introduced, she said,

"To continue the conversation, which I interrupted, Robert Browning's poem, 'Saul,' is a beautiful representation of the way the idea of Christ came to David. Have you read it?"

"No," said Alvin.

"I have," said Jennie, "and I cannot make anything out of it."

"Why," said Miss Somerville, "I have found some of his poems obscure, but this one was perfectly clear to me at first reading."

"If it is not too long," said Alvin, "I wish you would read it aloud. Twok tells me you are such an excellent reader that it is a real pleasure to listen to you."

Miss Somerville took a book of Browning's poems from the book-shelf and read the poem through.

"It certainly sounds very pretty as you read it," said Jennie, "but I can't say that I exactly understand it, even yet."

"I will try to explain it," said Miss Somerville. "There is David in the early morning, watching his flock in the open air and talking to himself. His voice to his heart. What a beautiful way of expressing the idea of talking to one's self? He is recalling to himself the events of the preceding night, his mind full of a wonderful new thought, that came to him while he was vainly trying to cheer king Saul, who had grown sick of life. He recalls to mind the image of the downcast king, who had wasted and desecrated the gifts God gave him, but had not yet lost his kingly bearing. While singing to

Saul, to console and cheer him, he sat at his feet, his head rising just above the king's knees, which were thrust out on each side of him. In the fervor of his singing the harp fell from his hands. He paused, and looked up in the king's face, to see what effect the music was having. Then Saul laid his hand on David's brow, pushed back the hair, and bending back the head so that the face was upturned, perused it as intently as men do a flower. As Saul scrutinized the face and looked into the eyes of David, the heart of the latter was full of love that beamed in his eyes and his face. This power of the human face to reveal love is the keynote of the poem. The king was greatly troubled; he had lost all hope; and David loved him with the same sort of devotion that true women have for their husbands. He thought, 'Oh, if love had the power to give happiness to the loved one, how happy would I make the king?' Suddenly the wonderful new thought comes to him. Every faculty that he has is a gift from God. The power to love Saul must be a gift from God. And yet he almost feels as if he loved Saul better than God does. He laughs at the absurdity of such a belief. Saul has been looking into his face and seen the love there. If he could only see God's love as clearly, then would he be comforted. Now he has it. No more harping, no more singing is necessary. He has only to say, 'O, Saul, it shall be a face like my face that receives thee; a man like to me thou shalt love and be loved by for ever; a hand like this hand shall throw open the gates of new life to thee! See the Christ stand!'

"The wonderful thought is this: That if he could, by looking into the face of Saul, show him his love, God, whose love is infinitely greater, and whose will is law, could embody his love in a human face, and that face is the face of the Christ. The idea is not new to us, but it was new to him, for that was many years before the time of Christ. Is it any wonder when he walks home for the first time after that grand thought has come to him, that the stars and the trees and the wild beasts seem to him to be awe-stricken at the new revelation?"

"It is clear to me now," said Jennie, as Miss Somerville finished speaking. "What do you think of it, Mr. Linklater?"

"It is certainly a grand poem, and I like Miss Somerville's explanation of it. But my time is up. I must say good-bye."

Alvin took his departure, saying that when he commenced his medical studies in Montreal he would be able to see them quite often. He ran back after starting, to tell Twok that his father was very anxious to have her spend several weeks at Broadglance during her summer holidays, and she said she would like very much to visit 'uncle Charles.'

CHAPTER IV.

THE evening sun shone on the windows of Joy Cougles' workshop, setting the panes on fire, as if they were opposing its entrance and a way had to be burned through; and then getting into the room somehow, in spite of their resistance, it filled the air with such a dazzle of microscopic brightness that millions of atoms, at other times invisible, danced and whirled as if being suddenly ushered into a new world, they were vainly trying to find their place in it. The window having been stormed and the invisible atoms made visible, the sun proceeded to stare into the face of a man who lay sleeping on his back on the bare floor, with his head pillowed in his clasped hands. Shining on his face it seemed to be examining his features, and just as the invisible atoms became visible in its light, so all the lines in the face of the sleeper were revealed almost as distinctly as if under a microscope. It was naturally a rather handsome face, with clear cut features, but the lines of dissipation about the eyes and mouth gave it an appearance of coarseness, which was increased by the three days' growth of beard and the swollen condition of the eyelids. As if wishing to raise those heavy lids and peep into the eyes within, the sun shone very strongly upon them, causing the sleeper to move his head uneasily, withdraw one hand from under it, and finally open his eyes. He lay there on his back for a moment, and then turning over raised himself partly on his hands and struggled to his feet. After which he peered around the room mistrustingly, as if fearing that some one was looking at him. Standing on his feet he appeared to better advantage than while lying on the floor under the scrutiny of the sunlight. He was tall and strongly built, and his clothes, which were of fashionable cut, set off his figure. Seemingly uncertain what to do next, he stood drawing his hand back and forth over his unshaven face, but after a moment's hesitation proceeded to build a fire in the forge. This was hardly done when there was a rap on the door, and he, continuing to stir up the fire with the bellows, and without looking around, said in a loud voice, "Come in." The door opened and Joy Cougles entering, advanced to the anvil and stood waiting until the man at the forge was ready to attend to him, when he offered his hand, saying,

"How are you, Dick Well?"

"Oh, it's you, is it?" said the other sullenly.

"Yes. How is business?"

"No business. It was a swindle, selling my uncle this shop."

"There was quite enough business when I left it to keep you employed, and the money I received was not so much for the business as for the house, land, furniture and tools, some of which were very valuable and could not be found in an ordinary blacksmith shop. When I sold it to your uncle I supposed he intended to run it himself, instead of giving it to you, who never thoroughly learned the trade. But if you have nothing to do, perhaps you will be willing to let me take charge of the shop for a month. I am longing to get hold of the hammer again. What do you say to that?"

"What'll you give?"

"How much do you want?"

"Fifty dollars."

"Rather high if you are not making anything out of it, as you say, but I'll give you that if you will allow me complete possession for one month."

"It's a bargain. When will you begin?"

"At once."

Dick watched eagerly as Joy took out the money, and after receiving his fifty dollars, said,

"I'll bet you ten dollars that I can guess how much you have left in that pocket-book."

"I never bet," said Joy, "but you can guess if you like."

"Sixty dollars," said Dick.

"Ten too much," said Joy.

"Well, you'd better bank it," said Dick as he left the shop, after arranging to return for some of his things, "or somebody'll steal it."

"I'm not afraid," said Joy.

Joy stood in the doorway as Dick Well took his departure, and watched the retreating figure until he saw another approaching on horseback. The new comer proved to be Alvin Linklater, who would have passed by without stopping, had not Joy whistled to attract his attention. Then, riding up to the doorway, he sprang from his horse, exclaiming, "Why, Joy Cougles! You here! It seems like old times."

Joy explained the arrangement he had made with Dick Well, and Alvin asked, "Do you feel as much at home in the old place as ever?"

"No," said Joy, doubtfully. "It seems different somehow."

"It is different," said Alvin. "It used to be the most cheerful looking place in Linklater village; now it is the most dreary. The old gravestone would look quite appropriate here now. It was rather odd about its being blown up; wasn't it?"

"What gravestone?"

"Your dog's gravestone."

"Has it gone?"

"Why, yes. I thought the doctor had told you about it. It was the talk of the village. This is the way the story goes: One Saturday night last winter, Dick Well had half a dozen young fellows in here, around the fire. They had whiskey with them, and were just beginning to get merry, when there was a loud explosion. The building shook, the plaster fell from the walls and ceiling, and several fragments of stone crashed through the window. They all started up, sobered by fright, and fled from the place. Next morning it was discovered that the big stone on your dog's grave had been blown into atoms. No one seems to know who did it, but some of the villagers believe it was Sam Slemmings. They say he poisoned your dog years ago, and that you carved on the stone: "Here lies a dog that was almost a man, murdered by a boy who is almost a beast."

"Yes," said Joy, "But I took it off afterward. I don't see what objection he could have to the stone now. Was he in the village at the time?"

"Yes. I think he was staying over Sunday. But what did you mean by saying that he was almost a beast? Did you really believe that Sam was as much of an animal as your dog?"

"Not exactly, but I had been wondering, for some time before, whether it would not be possible for a man to lose his spiritual nature altogether and become a mere beast."

"What do you think about it now? Twok was saying that you believe in the ultimate annihilation of the wicked, but when she spoke of spiritual death I thought that, of course, it would be either simultaneously with or subsequent to the death of the body. You don't believe that the man ever continues to live after his spirit dies?"

"I don't believe anything about it. Of course I don't know, but I have sometimes thought it might be possible, although improbable."

"The spirit, then, would be merely an essence without form?"

"Not necessarily. Sometimes my body weighs more than at other times. If I eat more than usual for some time, it will increase my weight. If I starve myself, my body will decrease in weight. The spirit may have form as the body has and yet waste away. After death, the body, as a rule, gradually decays and is resolved into various gases, losing its shape. Sometimes the change takes place more quickly.

Throw a live man into a blast furnace, and in a moment his body will have vanished completely. The spirit may waste away for want of spiritual food and gradually die. I can imagine that the commission of some vile sin might annihilate a man's spirit as completely and as quickly as the heat of the blast furnace would his body. You have heard, no doubt, of men committing assaults on women and little girls so vile, so brutal, that it is hard to imagine that they are anything more than beasts. They should be exterminated like wild beasts anyhow. It makes my blood boil to hear of men, guilty of such crimes, being punished by a year's imprisonment. I have no belief as regards annihilation of the spirit: it is merely a supposition, of course, incapable of scientific proof. But of this I feel certain: it is possible for a man to raise himself more and more above mere animals as he grows older, and it is possible to so indulge the animal passions as to deaden all the higher and nobler sentiments and impulses."

"To return to Sam Slemmings. He has improved, hasn't he?"

"In some ways he has greatly improved, but if the stories told of him are true, more than one life has already been ruined to satisfy his animal nature."

"Are not some men born with stronger spiritual natures than others?"

"Yes. I think it was partly that thought which permanently changed my feelings toward Sam Slemmings, whom I almost hated at one time. My feelings toward him became so bitter that I could not even wish him to become good. Twok held up the mirror to me and showed me how blackly wicked I was getting to be, and I prayed earnestly that night that I might overcome myself. I had not prayed for a long time before."

"You think, then, that your prayer was answered in that case?"

"I would not like to say positively that the prayer was

answered. The change in feeling may have been merely the outcome of the strong effort of will that enabled me to put my heart into the prayer, or it may have been due to the softening influence of a higher power, coming to aid me in fighting the deviltry in my nature. That is one of the things I don't know, and which nobody can know. The prayer did me good anyhow. But as I was saying, after the struggle was over I began to think that Sam was not so much to blame for his nature as his parents were, and I have made many excuses for him on that account."

"Then one child is born with strong spiritual impulses, and another with weak ones. The first becomes a noble man, and inherits eternal life; the second becomes more and more degraded, until he is annihilated. Isn't that very unjust?"

"No. Every man has the power to try to do right. It may be harder for A. to resist temptation than for B., but the mere act of trying to resist strengthens the character. B. seldom has to make an effort, consequently, he is more likely to stand still or advance slowly. A., always obliged to be trying, is of necessity always growing stronger in character, and gaining on B., and if each resists every temptation that comes to him, they will ultimately stand on the same plane. The degree of effort required to overcome temptation exactly measures a man's weakness, and the greater the effort, the greater is the accumulated spiritual power produced by it."

"But suppose A. does not try very hard; then he retrogrades and is finally annihilated, while B., making no greater effort, lives on."

"Well, even so, A. is in no worse condition in the end than if he had never been born. He is reduced to nothing. I can see no injustice in that. It is far better so, than that we should all be mere machines, so constructed that we could not be otherwise than good. There would be very little nobility in a human good-action machine."

"Very few men would be frightened into being good by threats of annihilation. The fear of hell fire would be much more effective in driving sinners into the fold."

"Well, it's a poor sort of goodness that is the result of fright. The man who refrains from evil doing simply because he is afraid of hell, is at best a spiritual dwarf."

"Then you believe ——"

"I repeat that I don't believe anything. I don't know, but it seems to me that if my supposition is correct, it does away with a great deal of seeming injustice. Moreover, it throws a new light on our relations to one another. I have said that God allows man, in a certain sense, to create himself by building up his own character. I will go a little further and say that if, by good counsel or kindness to any of our fellow beings, we induce them to try to do right instead of doing wrong, and so save them from annihilation, it is the same in effect as if we had created them. To create a human being! Think of the glory of it! I have very poorly expressed the idea I have in my mind. I may be able to work it out more fully and clearly some time."

"You talk now as if you believed it. You don't merely say 'perhaps.' You speak in terms as emphatic as any minister could use in preaching hell fire."

"Well," said Joy, laughing, "if so, it was not intentional. Of course I don't know anything about it, and I have never made a study of metaphysics, so my reasoning may be at fault. But the sun has long ago gone down. I have had nothing to eat and am getting hungry."

"Come home with me," said Alvin. "You won't get anything fit to eat here."

"Thank you. I think I will."

* * * * * * * *

The setting sun shone into many other rooms that summer evening. It got through the half closed blinds of the window of a room over a certain saloon on Broadway, Buffalo, gleaming brightly on a heap of greenbacks and gold coins, which an old woman was counting on the table, and looking inquiringly into her face. As the sunbeams got into her eyes she swept the money into a bag which she held in her hand, and turning around hurriedly, as if to address some one behind her chair, said in a whining tone,

"I didn't teach her any wickedness. It wasn't my fault that she run away. You said I could have half, and I was goin' to give her the rest."

There was no one else in the room, but for some minutes afterward the old woman writhed and groaned, as if she were struggling to free herself from some one who was torturing her. At last she fell exhausted on the floor, still clutching in her hand the bag of money, and lay there for half an hour or more. Then, recovering, she took from her head a coil of false hair, and laughing softly, fastened the bag inside it and replaced it on her head, saying,

"They think I'm gettin' vain, wearin' such a heap of false hair, but they don't know where I keeps my money."

She put on a hat over the wig, and, tottering to the door, went down stairs to the street. Just as she reached the sidewalk she fell in a fit, and a curious crowd soon gathered round. They were pushed aside by a tall man, who said,

"It's crazy Meg. I'll carry her to her room."

He took the old woman in his arms and carried her upstairs again. She had regained consciousness before they reached the top of the stairs, and as he opened the door, which she had neglected to lock, said,

"Don't let 'em in, Jake. You're the only honest one."

"I won't," said Jake, locking the door to keep out the crowd and placing her on the bed.

"I'm dyin', Jake," she gasped. "Take off my wig—the money's in it—it belongs to Twok—take it to her—don't let anyone see it."

He took the false hair from her head, and removed the bag of money.

"Hide it," she said, "or they'll steal it."

She watched him eagerly as he put it in one of the large pockets of his coat, and then closed her eyes, wearily murmuring, "I didn't teach her any wickedness," and when the doctor, who had been summoned by one of the crowd, entered with a policeman, crazy Meg was dead. Their attention was drawn first, not to the old woman, but to Jake, who had been seized with a violent fit of coughing after opening the door for them, and had seated himself on the edge of the bed.

"Why, my man," said the doctor, "you need me more than she does. We must try to do something for that cough."

They turned to examine Meg's body, and when the doctor looked up again Jake had disappeared. He had left the room so quickly and so quietly, that the doctor, matter-of-fact as he was, found his heart beating more rapidly than usual as he said to the policeman, after looking around the room,

"What has become of that man who was sitting here coughing a moment ago?"

"I thought he was as near dyin' as the woman," said the policeman, "but he must be uncommon full o' life to slip out o' here while our backs was turned. Guess he was shammin'."

"No sham in that cough," said the doctor.

The policeman hurried to the door and asked the crowd at the foot of the stairs if a man had passed out.

"Yes," was the response.

"Where did he go?"

No one knew.

CHAPTER V.

JOY had been anxious to secure his old shop for several reasons. He felt that the work would do him good after his term of study; he had an idea which he thought might lead to a valuable invention if he had an opportunity to work it out; and he wished to have an excuse for being near to Twok while she was spending her holidays in Linklater. So when Twok, coming home two weeks later, drove past the shop with Mr. Linklater, she heard the hammer pounding out her name in the old way. He had sent her a letter the day after his arrival in Linklater, telling her that he was working in the old shop again, and had received in reply the following letter:

MONTREAL, June 28.

DEAR JOY,

It seems so selfish for me to be living in luxury while you are hammering away in the old shop. Will you not let me repay you the money you spent on me during the years I lived with you and your dear mother? To pay you for your kindness would be impossible: all my fortune could not begin to do that. But if you had the money you have spent on me, you could finish your university course without any hard work. My first thought on learning that I was to be quite rich was that I would be able to repay you in part, but when I spoke to Dr. Somerville about it he said: " No, I want to see what the boy will do with himself. I love him as dearly as if he were my own son, and you may be sure that I will never see him starve. But give him a chance to show some pluck. If you begin to coddle him now, we will never know what he is worth. Let him alone. I want to have the pleasure of seeing him conquer the difficulties in his way. I am not going to be robbed of my hobby just because you happen to have some money." I hardly knew whether to laugh or to cry. I know he would make great sacrifices for your sake, but he seems to think that the more trouble you encounter and the more difficulties you overcome, the nobler your character will be. For my part I think you are quite good enough now, and it seems a shame that the best years of your life should be wasted just in order to keep Dr. Somerville's absurd hobby horse alive. A year or two saved now may make so much difference in your life, for there may be many opportunities for advancement which will be lost if you wait to earn money to carry you through the university. I know, for your mother told me, that you were studying and saving to go to the university when I came to you, an ignorant, neglected child, and you spent your time and money in educating me instead of yourself. I feel sure that but for me you would already have finished your university course, and I will be quite unhappy in thinking that I have been a drag upon your life, unless you allow me to do something for you now. I am going to Linklater in a few weeks for my holidays, and will spend the first eight or ten days with the Linklaters, as my uncle and cousin are going away for a trip later on. The remainder of the time will be spent with Dr. Somerville, and I expect that Miss Somerville will be there, too, during the latter part of my stay, so you will have an opportunity to make her acquaintance.

Yours sincerely,

TWOK TRENWITH.

Twok had carried this letter in her pocket for some days, scarcely knowing whether to send it or not, and had only dropped it into the post office the day before leaving Montreal, so that Joy had received it the morning of her arrival. He was now discussing with himself a question that had caused him much disquietude since the death of Mr. Trenwith. Was it right for Twok to keep the money so dishonestly acquired by her grandfather? On the one hand he argued that it would be impossible, after such a lapse of years, to make restitution; but on the other hand, he could not think that it was right for her to profit by her grandfather's wrong-doing. He had no doubt that she would wish to give up the money if she knew how it was obtained, but he asked himself, "Will it be worth while to cause her pain by making known her grandfather's crime, merely for the sake of observing the principle of honesty, without benefiting any one in particular?" He soon forgot his work and sat down with his head on his hand while he thought. He was so absorbed that he did not hear the door quietly open, nor notice Dick Well enter on tiptoe, advance across the shop to his bedroom, and conceal himself in a closet off the room. The sun had long gone down when the debate was concluded, and the decision was, "She must give up the money."

Having come to this conclusion he set about preparing his evening meal, but was interrupted by a feeble rap at the door, and opening it, was surprised to see the pale face of Twok's friend, Jake. He was about to invite him to enter, when the man staggered and fell, the blood streaming from his mouth. Joy lifted him in his arms, and carrying him to his own bedroom laid him on the bed.

"What have you done with my child?" was Jake's first exclamation on recovering consciousness.

"I will tell you all about her," said Joy, "as soon as you are better."

"Is she dead?" said Jake.

"No. She is alive and rich."

"Rich!"

"Yes. Her own father found her. He had been hunting for her for years. He was rich, but died very soon, leaving her all his money. She is living in Montreal. When you are better I will tell you more, but I think I had better find some one to send for the doctor now."

"No, no. I'll die before you get back if you leave me. I've walked—nearly all—the—way—from Buffalo—to bring her the money Meg left. It belongs to her. It's sewed in my shirt. Give it to her."

The dying man closed his eyes and was silent for a moment. Then he murmured to himself, "She wont be disgraced by me now. Nobody'll know that we had the same name." After another brief silence, starting up, he half raised himself, and catching Joy's arm eagerly said,

"Bury me alone—I don't want no funeral—it will make such a fuss—bury me somewhere that nobody'll know but you an' her—you'll tell her where it is, an' she'll plant flowers on my grave. Don't tell anyone else that I'm dead—she was the only one that cared for me—all the rest despised me 'cause I was born wrong—came into—world—wrong way—would have gone to heaven—wrong—way—only for her. Promise?"

"I promise," said Joy.

Jake closed his eyes with a little sigh, and Joy, leaning over him pityingly, saw that he was dead. He had left his poor, worn-out, earthly body, and was born into heaven in the right way.

Joy sat beside the body for some time, with his head in his hands. He very much disliked to bury the body himself, and knew he ought to inform the authorities, but he had promised Jake to carry out his dying wish, and after all, what did it matter to anyone how or where this poor man, whom everybody had neglected, was buried. He and Twok would know, and they would make a beautiful flower garden over his grave. This was a most foolish conclusion, and yet Joy Cougles was not a fool. Sensible people sometimes do very foolish things. There are occasions in the life of almost every man when he loses his mental balance, and it depends altogether upon the circumstances in which he is placed at the time, whether his foolishness will ruin him or not. The circumstances were very unfavorable to Joy just then.

Having decided to fulfil his promise he felt Jake's shirt, to ascertain where the money was concealed, and finding it over the heart, cut the shirt open with his knife and took out Meg's leather bag. This he transferred to his own pocket, without counting the money, and then made preparations for burying the body. Next to the blacksmith shop was a vacant lot which still belonged to Joy. It was here that his dog Lion was buried, and he decided that Jake's body should lie there, too. Taking some large boxes in which he had packed his books, to the shop, Joy proceeded to make a coffin. He had once mended Jake's shoes, although he was never apprenticed to shoe-making, and had done the job most satisfactorily, and now he shaped a coffin with the same facility. He thought as he worked of that other time when Jake had sat by the fire with Twok at his side, looking admiringly at him as he worked, and now he wondered whether Jake's spirit would care what sort of a coffin his body had, and if so, whether he could be looking on at this job, too. Thoughts of Jake naturally led to thoughts of Twok, and suddenly he found himself hammering the name of Twok. He was not at all superstitious, and yet he could not help shuddering at the thought that he had hammered Twok's name while making a coffin. At last the work was done, the coffin carried into the bedroom, and the body placed in it. Then he had to dig a grave, and he cautiously looked around in every direction before commencing this work. The hour being late and the workshop some distance from any other house, no one was in sight and he thought it safe to go to work. If anyone did come it would be rather awkward, but still he thought the matter could be easily explained.

While Joy was at work in the shop, the man in the closet had come out and watched him from behind the bedroom door. When Joy returned to the bedroom he returned to his closet, and while Joy was digging the grave he again came out and seated himself on the coffin. He had entered Joy's bedroom intending to steal his pocketbook, but now a darker thought was in his mind. "I have him tight," he said to himself. "I can swear that I saw him murder the man, rip open his shirt, take the money, make him a coffin, and then bury the body. It will take him some time to dig the grave, and here is his knife. I can make the evidence stronger still."

He took a screw-driver which Joy had laid down and unscrewed the lid of the coffin, stopping every now and then to look out and see that Joy was still at work. Then taking Joy's knife he plunged it into Jake's heart, and having screwed on the lid of the coffin went back to the closet. When Joy returned to the room he hesitated for a moment, half determined to open the coffin and take a last look at Jake's face. Had he done so, and found his knife in the body, the affair might have had a different ending. But reflecting that time was precious, he dragged the box with difficulty to the grave and buried it, making a large bed over it, as if it were intended for flowers. Then returning to the house he sank exhausted on the bed. As he did so Dick Well stepped out of the closet and said,

"You are the coolest murderer I ever came across."

"What do you mean?" said Joy, turning white with astonishment and alarm.

"Don't try to fool me. I saw it all. I saw you plunge your knife into his heart. I saw you steal his money. I saw you make his coffin. I saw you bury him. I am not a murderer like you. I wouldn't kill a man for his money, but I am not above saving you from the gallows now that the deed is done. Go halves with the money and I am your chum. If you don't, I'll see you hanged for murdering the poor man. I was in the closet when you did the deed and afterward crept out and saw you making the coffin."

"If you were there you know that he died a natural death, that he told me to take his money, and that I buried him in this secret way at his own request."

"I know what I saw, and all the circumstances are against you. When they open the grave they will find the coffin made of boards with your name on them. They will find the pocket in his shirt ripped open and the bag of money gone. They will find your knife in his heart. I mean business. That's what I say."

"You are right," said Joy, "in saying that the circumstances are against me; but one thing is certain: examination will show that there is not a wound about the body."

"Your knife is sticking in his heart now," said Dick. "I unscrewed the lid of the coffin while you were digging the grave and saw the knife sticking in his heart. Sticking in his heart is what I say."

Joy looked around for his knife which he knew he had left there. Then he understood what Dick had done.

"You can't frighten me into bribing you not to lie," he said.

"I am too tender hearted to take you at your word. I don't wish to see you hanged. I'll come and see you in the morning. It will soon be broad daylight. In consideration for your health I won't keep you longer. What with your butchering job, making a coffin and digging a grave, you must be very tired and in need of sleep. I will watch to see that you don't run away."

He made a mocking bow and left the place. Joy seated himself at the table with his forehead pressed against it. He got up in a moment intending to go to Dr. Somerville for advice, but sat down again, saying to himself,

"No, with his absurd way of looking at things he would probably consider it my duty as an ideal man to conquer my objection to being hanged."

As he resumed his seat he looked toward the window and saw Sam Slemmings looking in at him with an expression of triumph on his face.

CHAPTER VI.

WHEN Carlock and Sam Slemmings were left in the cave together after Twok had been informed of her father's death, they stared at one another savagely for a few moments, and then Carlock silently motioned to Sam to ascend the ladder, and he obeyed, scarcely knowing why he did so.

On reaching home Sam was welcomed by his father, who was growing very proud of his "lawyer son," as he called the young man.

"I want to ask your advice, Sam," said Mr. Slemmings. "You know them Linklaters never was much at makin' money. They owned all the country round here at one time, and now it's nearly all got into other people's hands, and I don't see as the Linklaters is any richer for it. Now, Mr. Linklater wants to sell part of his ravine. Goin' to invest in some western 'spec,' and wants a little more cash. There's lots of good buildin' stone in that ravine, and a good many cords of wood. Seems to me it would be worth what he asks, $1000. What do you say?"

Sam was about to suggest that Toronto property was more likely to increase in value, when it occurred to him that Carlock's house and cave were in this ravine, and he at once urged his father to buy the land. The purchase having been made he persuaded his father to deed to him the section of the ravine in which the cave was located, and afterward derived considerable satisfaction from the contemplation of Carlock's probable dismay upon being turned out of the cave. But some weeks elapsed before he was able to leave

Toronto to carry out his project of evicting the old man, and when he did visit Linklater he found that all the villagers were talking about Carlock's disappearance. He searched the cave carefully, inspecting every corner. It was so small that this did not occupy much time. What interested him most was the bedroom in which Twok had slept. With its costly furniture and tasteful decorations, it presented a strange contrast to the rest of the cave. He tried to open the big blue boxes, but found them securely locked. As the months went by and nothing was seen or heard of the village crank, Sam concluded that he was dead, and began to congratulate himself on the fact that no one excepting himself and Twok knew of the existence of the cave. He dreamed about it nightly, fancying himself in all kinds of strange situations, some of them so absurd that he laughed over them when he awoke, and others very realistic. There was one dream which recurred to him constantly, with many variations, but always the same in substance. He and Twok were in the cave together, and she was his prisoner. In another dream that often recurred he was opening the big blue boxes in the cave, but always awoke before he discovered what was in them. He often thought about these boxes during his waking hours, as well as in his sleep, and determined to force them open as soon as he had an opportunity to visit the cave again.

Meanwhile he made a discovery which turned his thoughts into a new channel. He had free access to the papers of Swingly & Swornly, and in looking over some of them one day found that all Trenwith's fortune was invested in a banking concern in a western mining town which was paying big dividends. A newspaper from the town in which the bank was located came to the office every day, and he began to read this paper with interest, although it was always more than a week old when it reached the office. One day, on opening the paper, his eye was attracted by the headline, "Gone to Canada," over a long sensational article describing a series of speculations on the part of the president and cashier of the bank, by which all the capital was squandered and nothing was left for the shareholders. "So Twok's fortune is gone," he said to himself as he finished reading the article, "and she will be penniless in a few weeks."

That night he was commissioned to go to Linklater and break the news to Dr. Somerville, and it so happened that about the time Joy Cougles was debating with himself whether Twok could honestly keep the money left her by her father, Sam Slemmings was sitting in the doctor's study, explaining how Twok's fortune had been squandered. The doctor listened to the story quietly, asked a few questions, said he would go to Toronto himself to talk over the matter with Swingly & Swornly, and dismissed Sam, telling him that he had a patient to attend to.

"I am very glad that the money has all gone," said the doctor, marching up and down the room after Sam was gone, "very glad. Now we can get back to old times again She will be better without the money, and I have enough for us all."

As Sam walked away he began to plan how he would inform Twok of her loss of fortune, and while she was cast down with the news tell her that she need not trouble for the future, for he would share his fortune with her if she would consent to become his wife. He expected her to be greatly impressed with this generosity. Indeed, he had taken not a little credit to himself in reflecting on the fact that the desire to possess her was no less strong than when he thought her worth one hundred thousand dollars. His thoughts were interrupted by the sound of approaching wheels, and turning he saw Twok and Mr. Linklater. Mr. Linklater bowed, but Twok took no notice of him, although he was sure she saw him.

"Confound her insolence," said Sam, grinding his teeth. "It will be different when she knows what I know about her fortune."

That evening after tea he started out, half intending to call on Twok, but changing his mind took a dark lantern and some tools which he had concealed under a bush by the wayside, and proceeded to the cave, intent on forcing open the big blue boxes, half expecting to find money or jewels in them. He succeeded in breaking open the boxes and found one empty and the other full of books. Then, tired and disappointed, he entered the pretty bedroom in which Twok had slept, and throwing himself down on the bed fell asleep. Again he dreamed that Twok was his prisoner in the cave. He had never before understood when he awoke why he kept her captive, but this time his dream was very clear on that point. He was holding her there because she would not promise to marry him, and this time she yielded. He had had this dream so often, that even while he slept he knew it was a dream, and it was the realization of this fact that awoke him. Lying there, awake, he said to himself,

"Suppose I should put my dream into effect. Of course it would be against the law, but I am determined to have her at all costs. Once get her here and I can make such mad love to her that she cannot resist me, for I am by no means an ugly man."

As Sam said this he arose, lit the gas, and surveyed himself in the mirror with much satisfaction.

"Besides," he continued, "the advantages of being the wife of a rich man could be set before her. She has become so accustomed to luxuries that she could never endure the life of a poor man's wife. Then she has her reputation to consider. If she refused to marry me after living here with me, she would have herself to blame for her ruin. In fact it would serve her right if I would not give her a chance to marry me afterward. I have borne more from her than most fellows would. She scarred my face when I was a boy, and now she is too proud to speak to me. Still, I am not such a fool as to risk the chance of getting into serious trouble, although as the existence of the cave is known to no one except me and Twok and old Carlock, and the old man is in all probability dead, there would not be much danger if she could be enticed here in anyway."

He laid down on the bed again, but could not sleep, and growing somewhat nervous decided to go home. He had to pass Joy's workshop on his way to his father's house, and when he saw Joy digging the grave he concealed himself to await developments, and was very much surprised a little later to see his former tutor dragging out a rough looking coffin. He waited until Joy entered the house again and then stationed himself at the window, which was raised a little way. He did not dare to keep his face there long for fear of being seen, but standing with his head bent down he could hear all that was said. He had no doubt that Joy was guilty, and when Dick left the room he could not resist the temptation to put his face to the window and look in at the supposed murderer. Joy, raising his head from the table, saw him, and jumping from his seat advanced to the window, saying,

"Now I understand this plot. You are at the bottom of it."

Sam had intended to depart without being seen, but now he stood his ground and said,

"You can't play that game on me, villain. I always thought you were a hypocrite. You, with all your purity of life, who used to preach to me about the danger of indulging in animal passions, are a murderer. You set yourself above me and set Twok against me, because I was a little fond of women and a little fond of wine and beer. You may say that what is bad in a woman is bad in a man, but the women themselves, who are the best judges, don't think so. The little sins I have been guilty of are the ones good women are most ready to forget and forgive, and the best and smartest men are generally a little fast in their youth. It shows spirit. But you are a murderer. There is no forgiveness for you. You have always hated me, and I am not sorry to see your hypocrisy exposed. Good morning. I will see you later."

He did not wait for Joy to answer, but hurried away, and ten minutes later was ringing the door bell at the house of Mr. John Boggs, justice of the peace. Mr. Boggs was somewhat annoyed at being called out of bed at that unusual hour, and looked out of the window with some impatience, exclaiming, "What's the matter now?"

"Matter enough, Mr. Boggs," said Sam. "It is murder."

"Hush!" said Mr. Boggs in a very loud whisper. Then shutting the window he crept down stairs, and opening the door only a little way, as if to keep out the murderers who might be around, admitted Sam.

"Oh, it's you, Mr. Slemmings," said Mr. Boggs, when he had lifted his lamp as high as possible in order to look at Sam, who was very much taller.

"Yes," said Sam.

"How did it happen," said Mr. Boggs.

"I was passing Joy Cougles house a couple of hours ago, when I saw him digging a grave in the vacant lot near his shop, and being somewhat curious to know what it was for, stopped to see what would happen. Soon he returned to the house and dragged out a plain board coffin, evidently of his own manufacture, which he buried. When he went in again I looked through the window and saw Dick Well, who accused him of having murdered a helpless man, stolen his money, made him a coffin and buried him. Dick had been concealed in a closet and saw it all. When I came away, Joy was trying to persuade Dick to conceal the crime, offering him half the stolen money."

"Who was the murdered man?"

"He had painted on the coffin in large letters the name, 'Jake Jakwok.' I remember my sister, who used to go to see crippled Mrs. Cougles sometimes, told me that the man who brought Twok Trenwith to Joy was called Jake Jakwok. It must be the same man."

"I can hardly believe this of Joy Cougles," said Mr. Boggs. "Still there is no doubt that his character has completely changed of late years. He was not the same man when he left here that he was a few years before, and, no doubt, he has gone from bad to worse in Toronto. But can you put this in writing, Mr. Slemmings? If I should go to bed now, I might wake up a few hours later supposing it only a horrible dream, unless I have something tangible to assure me of the reality."

Mr. Boggs brought pen, ink and paper, and Sam expressed his willingness to make a written statement. He hesitated a moment before writing the statement that he had heard Joy bargaining with Dick Well to conceal the crime, and then finishing, hurriedly signed his name.

"I would suggest," he said when Mr. Boggs had read it over, "that a watch be placed on Cougles' house at once."

"Yes," said the magistrate, "an inquest will have to be held."

After leaving the house of Mr. Boggs Sam took the road leading to Broadglance, and when the sun began to appear in the east like a great ball of fire, he was standing beside the wreck of the old elm tree looking toward it. He looked at the sun, and the sun, which shines alike on the just and the unjust, shone on him, but neither was thinking of the other. If the sun could have thought: if it could have looked into his heart and seen the evil passions which filled him at that moment, it would have discriminated for once and, concentrating all its blazing fury, scorched him out of existence.

Men seldom, if ever, deliberately determine to be wicked. They deliberately do wicked things, but they make excuses for themselves. A man likes no better to seem wicked to himself than to survey an ugly face in a mirror. Bad men are probably often more eager to justify their conduct to themselves than to other people. They attribute their sinfulness to their peculiar circumstances, and say that other men would yield if similarly tempted. If they think of God at all in connection with the matter, they either imagine Him to be a harsh, unjust Being whom it is impossible to please, and who will delight in tormenting them, or else suppose that He will compassionately make allowances for their temptations and their animal impulses while in the body, and, overruling all natural laws, place them in a quiet corner of heaven where it will be impossible for them to do wrong, and give them an opportunity to grow in grace. Sam Slemmings was no exception to the rule. In his own eyes he was a pretty good fellow, and could not be blamed for sinning a little when unjustly exposed to temptation. Was it his fault, he asked, that he dreamed every night of having Twok in his arms until he could no longer resist the temptation to possess her, willing or unwilling? Anyhow, he was sure he was not half as bad as Joy Cougles, who had murdered a sick man for the sake of his money. The supposed murder of Jake had aroused in Sam no feeling of horror or pity: it had only furnished him with an excuse for carrying out a plan of abduction, which he was revolving in his mind when he found Joy digging the grave. Twok's ill-treatment of him was rankling in his mind, and mingled with a strong animal desire for possession of the beautiful woman was a determination to take revenge. The abduction of a woman seemed to him a very small sin compared with the murder of a man, and at that moment when the refreshing morning breeze, the singing of the birds and the glory of the rising sun should have filled his heart with noble impulses, he was trying to devise a scheme to effect Twok's ruin in case she should continue to reject his proposals after hearing of her loss of fortune and Joy's crime. His thoughts were interrupted by hearing a footstep, and looking up he saw Twok. She had not seen him and he had time to conceal himself in a summer house that had lately been built a few feet away, before she reached the spot.

She stood beside the shattered trunk for a few moments, and then began to descend the path leading to the old quarry and deep pond in the ravine. If she had known the whole story of her mother's connection with that spot; if she had heard the story that Trenwith told to Joy, or had known what Alvin saw in his dream, she might have been superstitious enough to have avoided the tree and the pond into which the top of the tree had fallen, feeling that the place was a fatal one to her family and could not be safe for her. . But she knew only so much of the story as her friends had considered it advisable to tell, and that was very little, so she went on and Sam followed.

* * * * * * * * *

"Twok, my darling, you don't know how I love you."

"Mr. Slemmings, you will make me hate you. Go home at once," and Twok stamps her little foot passionately.

"I will not leave you until you promise to marry me. You despise me because you think you are rich, but you are not rich. Swingly & Swornly have charge of your affairs, and I know all about their business. The bank your father's money was invested in has failed, and you will have nothing. My father has made heaps of money lately, and I will have most of it some day. In the meantime he has given me some money to invest for myself, and I have bought property that will double in value in a short time. As my wife you will have every luxury, and every whim will be gratified, and you will have for a husband a man who loves you so madly that he would even dare to violate the law to secure you."

"Mr. Slemmings, you may be speaking the truth, but I would rather starve to death than marry you. Let me pass, sir."

"You think that blacksmith will marry you, but if you marry him you will be the wife of a murderer."

"No, Mr. Slemmings. You are so wicked that you ought to be killed, but he is too good to kill you. He doesn't hate you now; but I do." This is said with another stamp of the foot.

"Let me go, sir. I am going home. Don't dare to touch me."

Sam catches her arm and holds her.

"No. You shall not leave me till you hear all. He will not murder me because he will never get the chance. He will be hanged for killing your old friend Jake."

Such a cry of pain and horror! Have you no pity for that pretty creature you hold so tightly, Sam Slemmings?"

"You don't believe it? Well, I saw him bury him. Another man saw him do the deed. Joy killed him and robbed him, because he thought you would not marry him unless he had money."

"I don't believe it. I wouldn't believe it if all the world said so. I know him too well. You are a lawyer and you may be able to make people believe it, but I would rather go to jail with him than live in a palace with you."

"I might be able to have the crime hushed up. I could hire the man to keep quiet. I will do so if you will promise to marry me."

"I am sure Joy would much rather be hanged than have me marry you. Oh, do let me go. I believe you killed Jake yourself."

"Look here, Twok. We are in a lonely place. It is early. No one can see. I will drown you in that pond if you will not marry me."

"Do you suppose I care for that? I have lots of friends in heaven. There is Joy's mother, my father and mother, and the poor old man who kept me when I was a baby. He said he would haunt Meg if she was bad to me. I hope he will haunt you. Then there is Jake, whom you murdered yourself, and Joy will be there after you get him hanged. Oh, I'm not afraid of being drowned."

"Twok, listen to me. I only said that to frighten you, but what I say now, I mean. I am determined to have you, and if you will not consent now to marry me, I will carry you off to old Carlock's cave and keep you there. I own the cave, Carlock is dead, and no one knows of the cave but you and me. I can keep you there without suspicion, until you promise to marry me, or until I get tired of you."

Sam Slemmings, what are you about? You were right enough when you said that a little smattering of Greek and Latin cannot hide a man's character when the real test comes. Not even a smattering of law can do that. Joy was right, too, when he said that this nameless passion that people call love is little better than lust, unless it is hallowed and purified by love. You never loved Twok, Sam Slemmings. You have had your selfish likings, but I don't think you ever truly loved any one in all your life. If you had there might be some hope for you now. You did have that nameless passion for Twok, but now it has degenerated into Lust. Lust in your eyes; Lust in your breath; Lust in the arm you throw around her trembling waist. She sees it and understands it, and is frightened now. But you will not carry her to the cave without a struggle. Why, she is stronger than you are, Sam Slemmings, great, powerful, lusty brute that you are. She struggles in your arms and throws you from her. You grasp her again. Oh, will no one come to her aid? Her beautiful dress is torn to tatters; her long hair, more beautiful still, has broken from its fastenings, and falling around covers you both. But you are no nearer than at first to the accomplishment of your purpose. She is struggling toward the edge of the pond. If she can drag you in she will go to Heaven and you will go to Hell; or can it be true, as Joy thought, that a man who never cultivates the divine part of himself will at last lose his spiritual nature altogether, and become a mere animal? Is that pure girl struggling now in the arms of a mere brute? It may be so; but whatever you are now, Sam Slemmings, man or beast, she is going to defeat you. You are on the very edge of the pond. There! Over you go together!

CHAPTER VII.

ALVIN Linklater arose early that morning, too, and looking out of his bedroom window when half dressed, heard a woman's scream. Jumping out of the window he clambered from the veranda to the tree, and from the tree to the ground, as he had often done before, and ran in the direction of the sound. Reaching the path that led to the ravine, and hearing the struggle below, he crept to the very edge of the embankment, and looking over saw his cousin and the beast. Alvin has never been able to remember whether he jumped over the embankment or clambered down the path ; but he does remember that a moment afterward he was in the water with the exhausted girl in his arms, swimming toward the only spot where a landing could be effected. As he carried his unconscious burden up the steep path, scarcely feeling her light weight, he looked anxiously at the white, still face, so different from the expressive one of Twok, and there was a great dread in his heart that she would never open her eyes again.

Mrs. Gerty met him at the door, and taking in the situation at a glance, directed Alvin to carry her into a bedroom off the kitchen, where they rolled her in hot blankets and rubbed her body until she opened her eyes. Then Alvin mounted his horse and rode to Dr. Somerville's house. Twok had asked him years before if he could ride fast. Now he did ride fast, and when Dr. Somerville knew that Twok needed him he did not " wait to count his buttons." He did all he could for her, but I think the strain of the struggle and the terrible fright would have killed her, or left her a physical wreck, if her woman's love had not come to the rescue. The first thought that came to Twok when she opened her eyes was not of herself, but of Joy. That saved her. She remembered the struggle, but her mind dwelt only on that part of it that had regard to Joy. Sam had spoken of buying off a man. Was he lying, or was there really a man trying to bring Joy to the gallows? That Joy was guilty she did not for a moment believe. She must see Joy and contrive some way to save him. That thought gave her strength. If they thought her ill they would not let her go to see him. She must show them that she was quite well. She got up and dressed immediately, and when they told her she ought to sleep, said,

"Why, I slept all night. Do let me sit up in an easy chair."

They did allow her to do that, and by the time Mrs. Somerville had arrived in a high state of excitement, she looked almost as well as if nothing had happened.

* * * * * * * * *

But what of the beast? He—it struggled in the water for a few moments, sinking and rising, and at last was sucked down to the mud at the bottom. If it had been an expert swimmer, instinct might have saved it, but Sam had never learned to swim. The thing lies there, half in the water, half in the mud. Man or beast, whatever it was just before it died, the expression on its once handsome face is beastly now. If the water could keep the thing down forever, how much better it would be! Sam's mother must never be allowed to look on that face. Press it down, bear it down, bury it in the mud. It would be mockery to read the Christian burial service over that thing!

* * * * * * * * *

What a wonderful institution the modern newspaper is, and what a place it occupies in the minds of men! Mankind in general may be divided into two classes; those who are trying to get their names into the papers, and those who are trying to keep their names out. Dr. Somerville's first thought was, "It must not get into the papers. We can not allow our dear little girl to be the talk of the country." So he himself wrote out an account of Sam's death, which he carried to the editor of the Linklater *Vindicator*. The editor rewrote it, made a few additions to suit himself, and it appeared in the *Weekly Vindicator* next morning as follows, under flaring headlines :

> A deep gloom has been cast over Linklater and the surrounding country by the sad death by drowning of Mr. Samuel Slemmings, son of our wealthiest citizen. It is conceded on all hands that he was the most promising young man that Linklater, prolific as it is of enterprising young men, has ever produced. Foremost in all boyish sports while he was a boy, as soon as he approached manhood he applied himself to study with extraordinary zeal, and soon matriculated in law. Ever since he has been vigorously prosecuting his studies in the office of Swingly & Swornly, Toronto. Yesterday morning, being home on a visit, he went for a walk at an early hour, and in order to obtain a good view of the surrounding country stationed himself on the edge of the bank above the deep pond on Mr. Charles Linklater's property. While admiring the scenery he fell over into the pond. Mr. Alvin Linklater and his cousin, Miss Trenwith, were walking in the garden at the time and ran to his assistance, but too late. Indeed, Miss Trenwith, in her anxiety to help the drowning man, fell into the water herself, and would have been drowned had not her cousin jumped in and rescued her. The young man's family have our heartfelt sympathy. The funeral will take place to-morrow.

This is the way it appeared in the Toronto and Hamilton papers :

> A LAW STUDENT DROWNED.
>
> LINKLATER, ONT., July 15.—A young man named Samuel Slemmings, son of Robert Slemmings, of this place, was drowned in a pond this morning. He had lately been studying law in Toronto.

How often a tragedy is concealed under a one line heading in a daily newspaper, and dismissed without a thought by both editors and readers!

"What a good thing is a lie," said Dr. Somerville to himself, as he walked homeward after giving Sam's obituary notice to the editor of the *Vindicator*. "I must get Joy to put on his thinking cap and tell me what a lie is. He says we mix up several different feelings under the name 'love.' I wonder do we give the name 'lie' to two distinct things. There are lies that are wicked, and the very telling of them destroys all one's manliness. But then there seem to be good lies—kind, loving, sacrificing lies—lies that prevent many heartaches and brighten whole lives. I have an idea that some wordmaker centuries ago unfortunately made the acquaintance of a very bad lie—a disreputable, malicious, sneaking, mean-souled lie, and the whole family of lies have suffered in reputation ever since. Such is the justice of the world. I do wish I had Joy here to explain the thing to me. What can be the matter with the boy that he doesn't come to see me? Surely he is not still angry with me. He has reason to be angry, I suppose, as I told him Sam Slemmings was a nobler man than he. Joy understood the brute better than I did."

CHAPTER VIII.

WHEN Mrs. Somerville had taken leave of Twok, Alvin came in to ask how she felt.

"Quite well, thank you," said Twok, "but how can I ever thank you for saving my life?"

"Oh, don't try to thank me. You saved my life once when you found me in the woods. Besides, I love you so dearly, Twok, that nothing makes me so happy as an opportunity to do you a service."

"Oh, Alvin, I am so sorry."

"There is no occasion for being sorry. It is only friendship. You are to me the heroine of a novel in real life. Just as in reading a novel, if it be intensely interesting, one is for the time absorbed in the joys and sorrows of the heroine; just as he likes to study her character and is happy in her happiness, so am I interested in you. If one can be so enchanted with an imaginary heroine, fancy the charm of a real one. I have never for a moment imagined that you could love me, and surely there is no harm in my having that sort of love for you. It is a pity if a man cannot love his cousin. A cousin is almost the same as a sister."

There did not seem to be any occasion for blushing at such a declaration as this, but nevertheless Twok did blush most confusedly, and looked so charming withal that Alvin thought if the hero of this novel in real life had happened to be there, he would have been possessed with an almost uncontrollable desire to take her in his arms and kiss her.

Recovering from her confusion Twok said, "Alvin, to you who are both cousin and friend I will confide what I would not tell to anyone else in the world. The book in which you are interested has now reached its most exciting chapter, for the hero is in great danger. Listen while I tell you."

She told him what Sam had said about a murder, and concluding said pathetically, "He has been so very kind to me, Alvin. Can you not help me to save him?"

"I have no doubt," said Alvin, "that Sam's story was pure invention, and that we will find Joy all right, but if it should prove true that anyone is plotting against him, you may be sure that I will do all in my power to get our hero out of difficulty."

"Take me to see him, Alvin, at once. He thinks I am in Montreal. I cannot go to him alone, but with you I can."

"Are you well enough?"

"Perfectly well. Look at me. Do I look ill?"

Assuredly the color of her cheeks did not belie her words, but Alvin said,

"Had you not better wait until to-morrow?"

"I couldn't wait. I feel as if something dreadful were happening to him."

"What could you do, anyhow?"

"Oh, I don't know, but I must see him."

"Well, put on your things while I hitch up the horse. We'll have to go out quietly or the folks will raise a row. We can tell them afterward that we went for a drive, but telling beforehand would spoil our plans. The tire of one of the wheels of my buggy is cracked, and that will make a good excuse for calling on Joy. I will drive somewhat recklessly as we near Joy's shop, and the tire will be sure to come off."

As Alvin went out to get the horse he said to himself, "I don't know what the folks will say, but in my opinion it's a mighty good thing that she is anxious about Joy, and it will be far better for her to be out riding with me than sitting in the house, thinking about that brute, Sam Slemmings."

After Sam's departure Joy had sat still in his chair with his forehead on the table, all the old bitter feeling against the enemy of his boyhood rising in his heart. He felt sure that Sam had plotted with Dick Well against him, and he asked himself what defence he could make against the testimony of two men with so much circumstantial evidence to support their story. But surely Twok would not believe it. He would not care so much what others thought if only she would believe in him. But no doubt Sam would do his utmost to poison her mind against him. As the thought of Twok believing him a murderer, and perhaps marrying his enemy, grew upon him, he arose and paced the floor excitedly.

"I would almost rather kill him than let him have her," he said, and taking up a chair that stood in his way he dashed it savagely against the wall, breaking it in pieces, although it was well made, for he was a strong man at any time, and passion doubled his strength. But checking himself with an effort of will he said, "Falsely charged with murder, you are yet a murderer in your heart," and without stopping in his hurried walk he prayed for help to overcome his hatred.

With returning peace of mind came the determination to face the worst at once, and putting on his hat again he started for the doctor's house. On reaching it he was told that the doctor had been called suddenly away, and so he returned to the shop. He then determined to make a written statement of what had occurred and take it to a magistrate, and he was busily engaged in doing this when Alvin entered with Twok. In the pleasure of seeing Twok, Joy forgot for a moment his desperate situation, but soon recollecting said, "Jake is dead and I have your money."

"Tell me about his death, Joy," she said.

Joy told the story, dwelling in detail on the death-bed scene, but touching very lightly on Dick Well's action, for fear of shocking her. He knew by the expression of her face as she listened that nothing could make her doubt his word, but he did not feel so sure of Alvin, and it was to him he looked for a reply when he said: "What do you think? You do not believe me guilty?"

"How can you ask, Joy?" said Alvin. "Of course I don't think you are guilty, nor do I think you need fear Dick Well. But I will talk over this matter with you after taking my cousin home. By the way, we cannot get home without your assistance. The tire of one of my buggy wheels is very badly cracked and will certainly come off before we get home, unless you will mend it for us."

The wheel was taken into the shop, and Alvin said that as his horse was restless he would have to go out and hold it, leaving Twok to amuse herself in watching the work.

Joy heated the iron and began to hammer away energetically. When a man is brimful of love for a woman it is very hard to control the impulse to tell her of it. Joy had no intention of declaring his love then, but in his fervor hammered it out as distinctly as if he had put it in words.

"What is the hammer saying, Joy?" said Twok.

"I cannot tell you while this black charge is hanging over me."

"Oh, Joy!" she said reproachfully. "I would not ask you at any other time."

"It is saying, 'Twok, I love you.' That is what my heart says every time it beats, and the hammer is only pounding an accompaniment to the heart. Must I stop it?"

"If you do, it will break my heart."

The hammer had stopped talking now and fallen to the floor. Both her hands were in his and the eyes did all the talking that was necessary for a few moments.

"I have been longing for a kiss for years, Twok," he said at last. "I have often felt that I would gladly give ten years of my life for one kiss from you. May I have it now?"

"If you think kisses are so deadly I think you had better

not," said Twok, but he stopped the words with kisses, and it was several seconds before she was able to say, "You will throw away so many of your years at this rate that you will have none left in which to love me. You really must finish your work at once, or Alvin will be angry."

The work was soon finished and then Joy said, "Twok, I must insist on your keeping away altogether until I am proved innocent. I will not have your name connected in any way with such a matter. Now that I am able to think with both heart and head I will certainly be able to outwit these fellows. Go home at once and Alvin will keep you informed."

Alvin entering at this moment said, "You know you can always rely on me, Joy. I will come to you again when I have taken my cousin home. Can I do anything for you now?"

"Yes. Take charge of Twok's money. I have not counted it yet."

"Why, here is Dr. Somerville!" exclaimed Twok.

"What do you mean by bringing this child here to-day?" said the doctor angrily, addressing Alvin.

"Why I am quite well," said Twok.

"Has she been ill?" said Joy, "or is it because you believe me guilty?"

"Guilty of what?" said the doctor in astonishment.

"Joy, there is a face at the window," interposed Alvin. The next moment the door opened and Mr. Boggs entered with Mr. Clarkson, the village constable.

"I am sorry to disturb you, ladies and gentlemen," said the constable, "but I have a warrant here for the arrest of Joy Cougles, on a charge of murdering one Jake Jakwok. Mr. Cougles will have to go with me, and we will also have to take charge of these premises."

"Let me know the meaning of this," said Dr. Somerville.

"I will warn you, Mr. Cougles," said constable Clarkson, "that anything you say may be used against you."

"I am not afraid of that," said Joy, "but, Dr. Somerville, I think that Twok should go home."

"Yes, Twok," said Alvin, "let us say good-bye to Joy. We can do nothing now but say that we know he is innocent ; but going home we can put our heads together and think of a way to prove his innocence. I will keep you informed about everything, and we can go to see Joy if necessary."

"Go, Twok, like a good girl," said Dr. Somerville.

Twok said good-bye reluctantly, and as Alvin helped her into the buggy, constable Clarkson followed to say, "Don't be alarmed, young lady. I don't believe he's guilty. He'll come out all right."

When she had gone Dr. Somerville said,

"Now tell me what's the matter."

Mr. Boggs told him of Sam's visit and statement.

"Confound the lying brute," said the doctor. "Tell them there's not a word of truth in it, Joy."

"But there is a word of truth," said Joy. "It is partly true. I did make the man a coffin and bury him, but I didn't kill him."

He proceeded to tell his story in spite of a second warning from the constable. When he had finished, Dr. Somerville's face was full of despair.

"You do not believe me guilty?" said Joy.

"No, but I have made an ass of myself when I thought I was doing a clever thing. I was just congratulating myself on a neat little lie I told about this same Sam Slemmings. Had I told the truth, his statement would have been so much waste paper."

"It is always best to tell the truth," said Joy. "All lies are not alike. Some of them do more harm to the character of the person telling them than to anyone else, but you can never tell what evil the most innocent looking lie may work. I don't mean that you should tell everything you know. But if people would take as much pains to tell inquisitive persons in a polite way to mind their own business, as they do to tell a lie, a great deal of trouble would be saved."

Thus having said, Joy prepared to accompany the constable. It was not until Alvin visited him in jail that he knew of Twok's morning adventure and Sam Slemming's death. There were tears on the faces of both men when Alvin finished the story.

"I could not help thinking afterward," said Alvin, "of what you said about the annihilation of the spirit. It hardly seemed that it could be a man that was struggling to ruin that brave and lovely girl."

"It is an awful thought," said Joy, "but the more I think of it the more probable it seems to me. Of course by annihilation I do not mean absolute reduction to nothing. I suppose the spirit cannot be absolutely annihilated any more than the matter of the body. It can only be reduced to its original elements or element, and reabsorbed in the Divine essence to be utilized for some new creation."

CHAPTER IX.

LINKLATER village was wide awake after many years of drowsing—wide awake and talking. Talking was not a novelty in Linklater, but then the talk was usually about nothing; now it was about something, and all the villagers were talking about the same thing. There were two things to talk about: the death of Jake Jakwok, and the drowning of Sam Slemmings; but by common consent it had been decided that one depended upon the other and that Joy Cougles was responsible for both. It was argued that if Sam Slemmings had not been kept awake all night watching Joy, he would have been sleeping in the morning instead of wandering near the pond, and that consequently, in killing Jake, Joy had also brought about the death of Sam. Very little surprise was expressed. All had noted a great change in Joy during the last five or six years. Then it was remembered by more than one that he had a very ugly temper when he was a small boy. "And see how he scarred Sam's face," was said.

Twok's visit to Joy's workshop with Alvin was a subject for much gossip. The question was, would she believe him innocent in spite of the evidence against him?

"There is a peculiar fascination in a murderer for some women," said a lounger.

This remark was received with great disapproval. Twok was a mystery to the villagers, but men do not readily believe evil of a lovely woman, and moreover, the *Vindicator's* account of her early morning adventure, far as it was from the truth, had aroused popular sympathy.

But the point most discussed was Dick Well's attitude. He had been arrested at an early hour on the morning of the tragedy, and at the hearing of the case before the magistrate had positively refused to make any statement. In view of Sam's statement to the effect that he had heard Joy offering to divide the money with Dick if he would keep silence, the magistrate, after hearing Joy's story, had deemed it advisable to adjourn the hearing to await the result of a coroner's inquest. Dick's silence seemed to bear out Sam's statement, and the popular belief in Joy's guilt was strengthened.

"There would be a lynching bee if this were in the States," remarked one of a group of men in Mark Kenney's grocery.

"Yes," said another, "and there ought to be one here."

There was a murmur of assent, but no one seemed disposed to lead a lynching party.

"Why is it that we never have any lynchings in Canada?" was asked after a long pause.

"Canadian law," suggested someone.

"Climate," said another. "There are no cyclones in Canada either. You'll find that lynchings are most numerous in the cyclone country."

"*Vindicator* extra, only five cents!" cried a small boy entering, and several copies of the paper were soon sold.

"Read it aloud," said a man who had not bought a paper. The grocer opened his paper and began to read in a clear voice the following article:

The types describing the sudden death by drowning of Mr. Samuel Slemmings were scarcely distributed when they were again required to announce to the public a blacker tragedy. The accident to Mr. Slemmings, it appears, was but the climax of a night of strange adventure. At an early hour on the morning of July 15, Mr. John Boggs was awakened by someone rapping at his front door, and looking out of the window saw the late Mr. Samuel Slemmings, who told him that a murder had been committed. Mr. Boggs hastened downstairs and opened the door for his visitor, who stated that while passing Joy Cougles' workshop at a late hour on the preceding night he had seen Joy digging a grave in the adjoining lot. He stopped to see what the matter was, and soon afterward saw Joy dragging out a rough board coffin, on which was painted in large letters the name "Jake Jakwok." When Cougles returned to the house after burying the coffin, Mr. Slemmings stationed himself at an open window where he could hear and see what was going on within, and while in that position heard Dick Well say that he had seen Cougles stab the man Jakwok to death, rob his body and bury him. When Mr. Slemmings left, Cougles was trying to persuade Dick Well to be silent, offering to give him half the plunder. Mr. Slemmings, at Mr. Boggs' request, made a written statement of what he had seen and heard, and then walked away. He appears to have wandered in the direction of the Linklater estate, where he was unfortunately drowned, as described in yesterday's paper. A watch was at once placed on Cougles' workshop, and both Dick Well and Cougles were shortly afterward arrested. The new-made grave was opened, and Mr. Slemmings' story was verified, for the coffin was there and in it a man's body, with Joy Cougles' knife sticking in the heart. At the hearing before the magistrate, Dick Well refused to make any statement, and an adjournment was had to await the holding of an inquest on the body.

The inquest began in Cougles' workshop at 10:30 this morning, before coroner Herbert, and the following jury: Albert Jackson, George Tomkins, Edward Nelson, James Vandusen, Thomas Sawyer, David Green, John Hopkins, Ebenezer Toombs, Charles West, Arthur Bend, Joseph Ryan and James Edwards. The first witness was Mr. Boggs, and his testimony with the statement of the unfortunate Mr. Slemmings has already been given. Joy Cougles was permitted to tell his story, and reiterated the statement made to the magistrate that the man Jake Jakwok had come to his house dying of consumption, had fallen down at his door, bleeding at the lungs, that he had carried him to his bedroom where he died after directing him to take from his shirt a bag of money belonging to Miss Trenwith, and begging him to bury him secretly, telling no one of his grave except Miss Trenwith. He had accordingly made him a coffin and buried him, after cutting the bag of money from his shirt in which it was sewed. Dick Well, who had been concealed in the closet, had charged him with murder threatening to blackmail him unless he divided the money. This he emphatically refused to do.

"What time elapsed between the man's death and the placing of his body in the coffin?" asked the coroner.

"Probably three hours," said Cougles. "It took me some time to make the coffin. Is it likely that I would have painted his name on the coffin, or indeed made a coffin at all if I had murdered the man? It would have been much quicker work to have buried the body at once."

The next witness was Mr. Carlock. His appearance created a sensation, for as is well known he mysteriously disappeared some time ago.

Mr. Carlock said: "I am conscious that my unsupported word will be held of little account here. I have lived in such a mysterious way in this village, and have prevaricated so often, that in order to show I am now telling a straightforward story, it may be necessary to tell you something of my early life. There is no thing particularly interesting in my history. Most of you know that I have a sort of hobby for collecting relics of crimes. That, perhaps, would be deemed sufficient reason for my part in this affair, but I will take you further back. I was born in an English manufacturing town, and apprenticed to a cutler. I worked hard at my trade until I was made independent by a legacy from an uncle. Having toiled for so many years, I determined to equalize matters by doing no more work during my life time. So I travelled a little, read a little, gambled a little, ate and drank a great deal, and grew very fat. At first my successes at the gaming table were so moderate that they only served to put me in a good humor without exciting me, but as years went by my luck increased and I scarcely ever made a venture without winning a large sum of money. Then I began to grow excited, to stake large amounts—and to lose. I was so confident that my luck would take another turn, that I kept it up until almost my entire fortune was gone. All the while I was growing thin with excitement and anxiety. At last, recovering my senses somewhat, I emigrated to Canada, and squatting in the Linklater ravine, quietly pursued my old business of knife-making in a small cave, which I found under the old miller's house which was reputed to be haunted and so safe from intrusion. I worked there secretly for reasons of my own until my cave was discovered by that sneak, Sam Slemmings. Then, having acquired a competence by the sale of my knives, and Linklater being usually a poor place to collect relics of crimes, I decided to move elsewhere. I have been living in the States for some months, but a longing to see the old place led me here just at the right time. Visiting my cave on the night of July 14, I was surprised to find Sam Slemmings sleeping there. I knew him well enough to believe that he was bent on no good, and so concealed myself under the bed to await his waking. When he awoke he began to talk to himself about what appeared to be a plan to kidnap a certain young lady. When he left the cave I followed him, and when he stopped to watch Cougles dig the grave I stationed myself at a window of the house to see what was going on inside. I saw Dick Well step cautiously out of a closet, unscrew the lid of the coffin, stick Cougles' knife in the corpse, and then screw on the lid again. As he bent over the body, I noticed a breast pin sticking rather loosely in his necktie. When he arose after screwing the lid on the coffin again, the pin was gone. I suspect that it dropped into the coffin. I noticed another thing. While he was unscrewing the lid of the coffin, the screwdriver slipped, inflicting a wound on his left hand, which bled freely, but not profusely enough to attract his attention. He did not seem to notice it himself. This may seem odd at first thought, but on reflection most of you will remember having discovered a bleeding scratch on your hand at some time without knowing how it was received. In this case the wound was worse than a scratch, but the excitement of the moment probably prevented the pain from being felt."

Dick Well, who had listened intently to the witness, at this point looked down at his hand, which was neatly bandaged, and every one in the room looked at him. To the surprise of all he now stood up, and, unwinding the bandage, displayed a slight gash. "It's true enough," he cried. "I did not know how I got it, and it kind of frightened me, for I thought perhaps they might think I killed him myself. Fact is, I didn't intend to have Cougles hanged. I'm not bad enough for that. I never intended to tell anyone whether he gave me part of the money or not, but thought I would frighten him so that he would divide equally."

"Then the statement of the last witness is quite correct?" said the coroner.

"Quite correct," said Dick Well.

"Go on with your testimony," said the coroner to Mr. Carlock.

"As to what followed," said Mr. Carlock, "I can only say ditto to Mr. Cougles. Everything occurred precisely as he has stated."

The next witness called was Alvin Linklater. He had received from Joy Cougles the bag of money belonging to Miss Trenwith. The bag was produced and emptied on the table. The coroner counted the money, which amounted to $1,200.

Dr. Wright and Dr. Smith were called at this moment to state the result of a post mortem examination of the body. They agreed in saying that the knife thrust appeared to have been made after death. The man was evidently in the last stage of consumption and apparently died of that disease.

"How can you tell the difference between a wound made before death and one made afterward?" asked the foreman of the jury.

"In the first place," said Dr. Wright, "if the wound had been inflicted during life there would be eversion of the edges of the flesh owing to vital elasticity of the skin. Then there would be much hemorrhage, probably of an arterial character with infiltration of blood in the surrounding parts. In the case of a wound inflicted some hours after death, either no blood is effused or it is of a venous character—that is, it may have proceeded from some divided vein. The blood is commonly liquid, and does not coagulate. The edges of the wound are close."

Dr. Herbert here produced a copy of "Taylor's Medical Jurisprudence," and read to the jury a number of passages corresponding with what Dr. Wright had said.

"The distinction between a wound inflicted soon after death," continued Dr. Wright, "is not so well marked, but in this case I think there is no doubt that the wound was inflicted several hours after death."

"Did you find anything in the coffin?' asked the foreman of the jury.

"Yes," said Dr. Wright, producing a large breast pin. "I think I have seen someone wearing this, too."

"It is mine," said Dick Well.

No one doubted it, for it was a rather costly pin, and Dick has always been fond of displaying it in the taverns, so that everyone present recognized it at once. It need hardly be said, that when the jury retired they did not argue about the verdict. All agreed at once that the man called Jake Jakwok had died a natural death.

In conclusion it is only fair to say, that while Mr. Joyce Cougles made a mistake in the first place in regard to the secret burial of his friend, he has acted in a manly, straightforward way ever since. The introduction to this article was written before the inquest, when the writer believed, with many others, that Mr. Cougles was guilty, and it may convey a false impression to those who do not read to the end. We trust that all will read the whole article in order that no mistake can be made. Without doubt, our old friend, Mr. Joyce Cougles—we like to call him Joy—was only guilty of an act of kindness in trying to carry out a friend's dying wish, and it is a shame that anyone in the village, remembering the noble way in which he cared for his crippled mother and his sympathy with those who were in trouble in by gone days, could believe him guilty of so black a crime as that with which he was charged. It is true that he was less intimate with the villagers of late years than formerly, but that we fancy was their fault, not his. We hope the old kindly relations will be resumed.

CHAPTER X.

OF course the hearing of the case before the magistrate after the inquest was only a formal matter, and Joy was at once set at liberty. Twok was as much pleased with Meg's bag of money as if she had never known what it was to be rich. Neither she nor Joy think of Jake as lying in his grave, yet they have planted flowers upon it, and Twok cares for them tenderly. Of the past life of Twok and Joy there is little more to tell. Of their future I am as ignorant as they themselves are. As Joy grows older and wiser, his opinions on certain matters which have been touched upon are likely to alter somewhat. That he will always be searching for the truth, I am sure: that he will ever find it is far less certain, but his opinions will probably be worth more some day than they are now. He and Twok are not married yet, and as Dr. Somerville is in no hurry to lose his adopted daughter they will wait until Joy can offer her a comfortable home. He said to her one day recently, "Twok, you have heard me tell exactly how I felt about you. How did you feel?"

"How like you to ask, Joy," she said. "You analyze all your own feelings and expect me to do the same with mine. Do you remember one day years ago when I was a little child I asked you how the birds could tell when the cold weather was coming. 'I don't suppose they can,' you replied. 'Then why do they fly south just in time to escape being frozen?' I asked. 'They cannot reason for themselves like men,' you said, 'and I suppose God impels them to go at the right time.' 'How kind of Him to care for them so,'

I said, 'but how do you suppose they feel when He impels them to go?' And you answered, 'I cannot tell for certain, Twok, but this is what I guess. The day is bright and sunny and the air pleasant and warm; all the world around them is just the same as usual, but they feel that something is wanting; they are not contented; there is a restless, uneasy feeling which they could not explain even if they were philosophers, which they are not, and so they fly away to find rest.' That was your explanation about the birds. Now Joy, I cannot describe how I felt all the time. Sometimes the thought of being loved by you made me feel very happy. That was when I thought you would tell me that you loved me so that I could let you know that I loved back, but at other times I felt as the little birds do when God impels them to fly away."

"I am not certain," said Joy, "that I would explain the birds' flight just in that way now, but I suppose that is your way of saying that marriages are made in heaven?"

"Why, I didn't think of that," said Twok, "but it does seem like it."

THE END.

Who is Santa Claus?

BY WATSON GRIFFIN.

(Written for the " Toronto News," Christmas, 1883).

The top of her head was just even with the counter of the business office, and when the business manager looked through the wicket to see who was speaking, he saw a pretty, upturned face.

" Is this where the editor lives ?" she asked.

"Well he doesn't live here exactly," said the business manager, " but he works here."

" Could I see him ?" said the child.

"The managing editor isn't here just now, but perhaps the exchange editor would do. Come with me, and I'll show you the way up-stairs."

The child took his hand trustingly, and a moment later he called from the foot of the stairs, " here's a little girl who wants to see you."

The exchange editor clipped an article from the New York *Sun* and called out " send her up."

He waited curiously after that, and listened to the patter of the little feet on the stairs, until a sweet child's face appeared in the doorway, and then he offered her a chair as respectfully as if she were a lady grown.

" Are you the exchange editor ?" she asked.

"Yes. What can I do for you to-day ? "

"Editors know everything, don't they ? "

" Almost everything," said the exchange editor doubtfully,

for he knew that a child's questions are often harder to answer than those of a man. And then he added, "what we don't know we generally know how to find out."

"Well," said the child, "why does Santa Claus give rich children prettier toys and more of them, than he gives poor little girls? Poor children need presents the most."

It was a hard question to answer. Should he tell the child who Santa Claus really is and so, in answering her question, dispel a charming mystery that has lightened and brightened the mind of childhood for ages? He remembered how he would lie awake when a child for weeks before Christmas thinking about Santa Claus, and then fall asleep and dream about him all night. And how he hung his stockings by the fireplace the night before Christmas, kissing mother good-night early so he could get up to feel his stockings before it was light and take them back to bed with him to guess what Santa Claus had brought until a light was struck or daylight came through the window. And how he would hurry to mother's bed-room to wake her and father up and show them what Santa Claus had brought, sure that they would be as surprised and happy as he was. He remembered, too, what a pang there was when they told him all about it, and how a certain charm went out of his life never to come back again, and he felt that he couldn't bear to see the pretty little face clouded. Somebody else would have to tell her. But what should he say? He could invent some answer if he had a little time.

"Could you wait until Christmas morning?" he asked. "Then I'll tell you all about it in the paper."

"Oh; thank you. I'll get the paper early, and ask papa to read it to me."

So she said good-bye and declared that she knew the way out when he offered to go with her. But when she had gone, his mind was not quite at ease, for he could not think of an answer to her question.

As the exchange editor sat in his room at night, smiling over an amusing paragraph which he had just clipped, he suddenly looked up and saw standing beside him a jovial-faced, grey-bearded old man, loaded down with toys. He had never seen Santa Claus, except in the shop windows, but he recognized him at once, and felt like shaking hands heartily with his visitor ; but he remembered the child's question, and said, " Have you any objections to being interviewed ? "

" None at all, but make your questions brief, for I have a long journey to make to-night," and Santa Claus sat down on a chair, placing his pack on the floor beside him.

" Why do you give rich children prettier toys and more of them than you give poor children ? "

" Ha, ha," laughed Santa Claus, " you want to know my secret, do you ? Well, I'll tell you. It is generally supposed that I buy the toys. I merely distribute them. You see for weeks before Christmas people are constantly making mysterious shopping excursions, but they never seem to buy anything. At least they never tell anybody what they buy. They go home with mysterious parcels under their arms, take them to their rooms and lock the doors. They have been buying Christmas presents, but they don't want anyone to know it, so they give them to me with directions, and go down stairs after dismissing me, looking as innocent as if they had been out walking in the bracing air merely for the sake of their health. Of course the poor people can't give me such costly toys for their children as the rich people do, but they love them just as much, and sometimes rich people give me an extra load of toys, and perhaps a turkey, and tell me to leave them in some poor man's house. If every rich man would do that way, the poor children would all be served nearly as well at Christmas time as the rich ones."

" Don't you think it is a bad practice to deceive children in this way ? "

" No, sir. Decidedly not. It's one of the few good old time customs that you have retained. Just notice the difference between a Christmas gift to an adult and a gift to a child. You generally proportion your gifts to the grown-up person according to what you receive from him. You think, 'I must make a present to this person or he'll say I'm mean.' Is it so with Christmas gifts to little children? No. They are purely unselfish. The feeling that prompts them is love and nothing else. The custom should be kept up."

Santa Claus lifted up his pack as the foreman of the composing room called out from the head of the stairs, "What are you doing down there? The printers are all waiting for copy. Hurry and send some up."

The exchange editor rubbed his eyes, and looking up found that Santa Claus had gone.

THE PROVINCES AND THE STATES.

BY WATSON GRIFFIN.

TORONTO: J. MOORE, 1884.

This little book of eighty-five pages, the main object of which is to show why annexation, or commercial union, would not be to the advantage of the Canadian Provinces, explains how the Dominion may have protection and free trade at the same time.

"It is marked in the main by sound wisdom, and contains several suggestions which, sooner or later, are destined to bear fruit." — *Montreal Gazette.*

"He writes plain English ; some of his reflections display acute thought ; and some ideas which are not new are presented in a new shape."—*Hamilton Spectator.*

"The author's style is rather strong and lucid than ornate, but the book is eminently readable and suggestive. Many of the most telling points made are thoroughly original, and the whole book has the impress of being written, as the religious phase has it, under deep conviction." — *Toronto World.*

"Here the reader will find in the smallest compass in which it was ever attempted to summarise such important matters, a vast amount of information concerning Britain, Canada, and the United States, all given in a form so condensed, yet so lucid, that page after page opens to you like the shelves of a warehouse, from whence you can, if you are satisfied with the goods, stock your mind with the precise article you want. The work is valuable and should be read, especially when at the expense of so little time it may be read."—*R. W. Phipps.*

www.ingramcontent.com/pod-product-compliance
Lightning Source LLC
Chambersburg PA
CBHW021804230426
43669CB00008B/633